A personal message to my family and friends

Especially to my daughters, Karen, Samantha & Sarah

Maybe after reading this book, you may understand what made
me do the things I did.

Only read it if you want the truth.

To Mum and Dad, thank you for being there for me forever.

My thanks to David Cashmore for his advice on the writing of my autobiography. When I contacted him, I was already on a re-write. I had strayed away from the original concept and finished the story on a downer. I had this feeling that I had failed in everything I had done.

He wrote these kinds words after reading the first draft.

"I'm not sure where you are defeatist.
I always thought you were very outgoing and accomplished.
And if truth be known, I always felt belittled by your abilities.
When I met you, you were successful in business.

You were able to do technical drawings. You'd built your own place in Spain.
You had the ability to paint and draw very well and sell your work.
You had the estate agency, and then the radio station going on.
You were certainly well-liked and socially very active.
My goodness, Norm, there are ten thousand men who haven't done half what you've done and are doing."

Thank you, David.

I would also like to mention and thank

Jennifer Sarduy, for her advice, passion, friendship and
John Marshall for his expertise in proof reading.

The intimate, true story of the life of a man who loved music and women and who wanted recognition.

This book tells it as it is, my visits behind the Iron Curtain during the Cold War, my search for recognition and the feeling of inadequacy in my life, following years of illness and missed education in infancy. My latter years are spent in Catalunya, living in a rural location on the banks of the River Ebro, enjoying a relaxed lifestyle, socialising, writing this book, composing the 'Last Song' and living happily with Georgina, my partner, friend and lover.

Music downloads associated with this publication can be obtained from www.normanjaymusic.com

"I always thought that Norman would make it big as a singer the first time I heard him in the studio. Always a pleasure to work with and professional to a fault."

**John Needham, music producer and
Director of Pennine Studios.**

"Dear Reader,

You're in for a rare treat, reading this book. When I read through it, I found the story captivating, interesting, educating, in places very funny, in others sad. It's all tied together with Norman's own personal experiences, his own music and performances, even his own radio station and the music of the day. All this while battling with work, love, constantly moving home, jobs and house building. Much more than most of us could achieve or would even want to take on. It's very special for me because Norman was a work colleague. I visited him at his homes in Devon and in Catalunya, I was an avid listener to Radio Catalunya, and I lived for over twenty years near the featured Webbington Country Club. It reminded me, as Norman's story unfolded, of some of the stars and wonderful music of the time and also of some of my own similar ups and downs in life, even in the same company.

Well done and very best wishes for the publication."

David Cashmore. *Canggu, Bali. Indonesia*

"Norman Jay is an entertainer, who through generations
has seduced crowds in many countries with bright,
energetic music as both a presenter on
radio and a talented vocalist in person. I have been pleased
to know Norman and share airwaves with him over the
years. A truly talented man I am proud to know."

Gene Arnold, veteran radio and TV presenter and

The Sounds of Philly pioneer.

"Always brought me the most challenging arrangements.
I am glad to have been part of Norm's rich tapestry
of ideas"

Lol Harris. Musician arranger, owner of

Lollipop Studios.

"Norman's audiences have been captivated by the
versatility of his
style and his clever re-arrangements blended with his
original songs."

George Bellamy, SRT records.

Disclaimer.

I had a manager called Dick Clarke.
Not to be confused with the American
Dick Clark
of American Bandstand fame
Also a manager for many American acts.

Quote
Songs are like handwriting,
they are instalments in an autobiography.
Each one opens a window to a man's inner self.
John Lennon

I have therefore included song lyrics in the book.

Table of Contents

I have a secret that only now I can reveal. I am not the person you think I am. No longer the pale, often bullied under-performer I used to be. I changed my name and developed into a more confident individual. Both people still exist however, and sometimes I forget who the real Norman is.

One has masses of determination, drive and ambition; the other with a short attention span, who just wants an easy life. One seeks recognition, the other a warm friendly bosom. Torn between a life of music, or a loving companion; can they possibly co-exist? Ever-changing like the weather, one can be winter, while the other is always summer.

Confused? *We haven't even started.*

I have often been asked over the years, "What is your favourite song?" My reply has always been "I don't have one."

How could I single out one song? It's impossible. Ask me to make a list of my top ten and it would probably be different every time.

Maybe this is a good time then, to analyse my musical taste and create a catalogue of artists and songs that have influenced and touched me over the last half century.

Everybody is different when it comes to musical taste. That's what makes music magical; a song can take you to a place of fantasy or return you to your distant past. Or, you could be the kind of person who buys or downloads an album religiously each month and plays it over and over again, until you know every note, every word.

Once done, you move on to the next purchase. This person is usually building up a library of a particular genre of music. Or it could be that at some stage during his teenage years a social event or a music era influenced him. Or maybe it was his social background that was the catalyst for his musical taste. It's fascinating isn't it?

 Looking back, I suppose my musical education started in the fifties, listening to the radio playing music as far back as the thirties. Now 2016, that's a period of around eighty years that I have been subjected to a plethora of music.

I have a passion for music, so let's define this particular passion. Do I simply love music per se, or does it merely indicate that I enjoy songs about love?

A songwriter often becomes a songwriter because of a personal experience; that moment when either anguish or that swelling of the brain, due to love or lust, fuels the creative cells and other parts of the body. This results in a song that touches your feminine side or reminds you of a special relationship.

Okay, so not in every case, but I do believe the majority of individual popular music composers start off that way. However, suppose you were a Beatle? You would of course develop a style influenced by your fellow musicians and the music trend at the time, but your finest songs would always be about a personal experience.

I found I had a voice when I was still in nappies I guess. This influenced my taste, just like a guitarist or a violin player would be influenced. Exposure and familiarity may also be a key factor in what makes a person like a particular song or performer.

So my first music was vintage, big bands and young band singers. Frank Sinatra caught my attention and an English guy called Anthony Newly, who became an award winning song writer.

I can hear you saying, 'Never heard of him'. He was married to Joan Collins and was a significant influence on a certain David Bowie.

When I started singing for family and friends as a young boy, I would sing, '*Love is a Many Splendid Thing*', and '*Once I had Secret Love*', made popular by Doris Day. Also, '*Moon River*' and '*Singing in the Rain*', songs from films I had seen on the TV and heard on the little brown box nestling in the corner of my room. I was just a kid, but I knew I could get attention by singing, so I did a little bit more practising. Elvis came onto the scene and I sang some of his songs. Then the Everly Brothers hit the scene, and the second ever record I owned was a 78rpm vinyl of '*Bye Bye Love*'. Loved that one, played it every day, until my Dad stood on it. Bye bye record. I knew that song inside out and gradually began to understand what made it sound so different. It was the unique blend of the closeness between the brothers and their guitar style.

The first record I bought was by Lonnie Donnigan, 'Skiffle', soon surpassed by rock & roll.

Bill Hayley was the first American artist to visit London, belting out his rock and roll music. It started a revolution in England, and soon UK performers were born, Wee Willy Harris, The Most Brothers, Tommy Steel, Adam Faith, to name a few. Young guys bought electric guitars, groups like The Tornados and The Drifters, soon to be called The Shadows, (who had to change it, due to the American group of the same name), became popular. Micky Most became an agent and impresario, so too did Jack Good. He produced the '*Oh Boy*' TV show, where a young guy called Cliff Richard, with a fresh-faced Billy Fury, The Dallas Boys and The Vernon Girls were featured, and a new generation of music listeners was founded.

I soon realised that out of all the singers, one in particular, seemed to sing like me. Ha! By that I mean I could sing along with him, even phrase like him. So I started copying his style. He quickly became very popular and because of his popularity, he was getting the best songs, which soon led to films, just like the King ,Elvis.

 Cliff Richard. His name was on every kid's lips. I was one such kid, sitting in the cinema in Manchester, The Odeon, Deansgate, to be exact, watching and listening to him, in the film, 'Summer Holiday,' along with screaming girls all around me. It was great fun. I was so totally in love with Una Stubbs, his co-star.

 Cliff was a sort of mentor, I guess, a role model, and why not? The other thing was, that most of the other up-and-coming singers stayed with the rock style, but Cliff, now in films, was singing ballads and arrangements in the style of the 40s and early 50s that I had become familiar with in my early years, whilst listening to the radio but with a new modern sound. This was me, what I identified with.

Did I want to be him? You bet your bottom dollar I did!

So the songs included in my first years as a solo performer, came from Sinatra, Bobby Daren, Elvis, Pat Boone, Perry Como, and of course Cliff.

I would adapt songs from female artists too, like Doris Day and Shirley Bassey. Any popular song of the day had to find a way into my set, including hits from The Beatles, The Searchers, The Hollies, Herman's Hermits etc.

I start my story at a low point in my life. Around the year 2000.

I had left my marital home, my wife, and children, some six years earlier, after almost twenty-five years of marriage, for the love of another woman.

That new relationship, once full of love and happy times, had sadly also recently ended.

I was not depressed, just confused. I was not a bad person and I

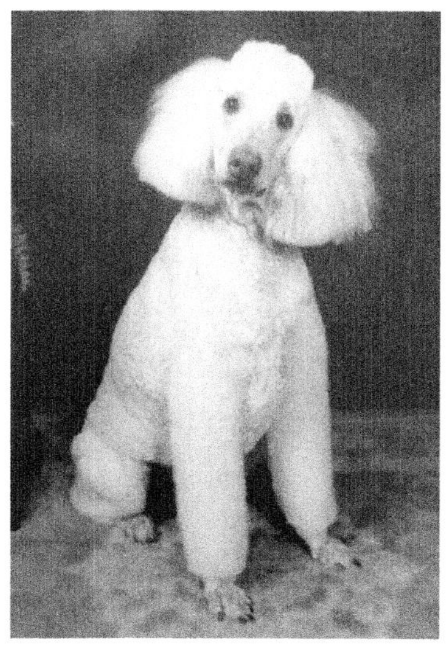

didn't like hurting people. The circumstances, that time, were a little easier for me to understand. However, when it came to the breakdown of the relationship with my wife, that was different. I was driven by ambition. I wanted success and I had married her too early in life.

So there I was, just me and my faithful dog Danny, starting all over again. He lived to the grand old age of seventeen.

15

Chapter 1

Single again, year 2000

"I have always had a lover and I have always let them down. It seems I always recover, and leave all the mess behind."

Words from a recent composition of mine. You should always listen to the lyrics of a song, they tell a true story!

I am standing inside a 1960s caravan that I have just purchased, with the intention of living in it!

It's extremely tired looking, inside and out - it should be bulldozed actually. The ceilings are bowed and stained, where the roof has been leaking. Brown damp patches form the most part of the decor, like a painting in water colour, and green mould is apparent around the old single-glazed, aluminium windows. The toilet and kitchen, obviously original, are functional and reasonably clean but these days at the start of the millennium, totally unacceptable. My eyes shift to the floor, a deep-pile, dark brown carpet, threadbare in places, covering the main area, and you can clearly see the depressions where the furniture had been positioned for the last twenty years. A set of wooden French doors, not an original feature, have obviously been recycled and cut down from their standard height, to fit into the side wall of the van, a nice touch in a way. An upgrade from years gone by.

The sun shines in through the old doors, illuminating the overgrown garden. I unbolt the double doors, step outside down some timber steps that almost collapse under my weight, totally rotten. I stand there silently in this overgrown wilderness, reflecting.

 I can't help but appreciate the beautiful morning. The dew glistens on the grass and the cobwebs, meticulously woven over the brambles, reach high above my head dancing and shimmering in the light warm breeze. My head tilts back to catch the warmth of the morning sunrise through the tall pine trees, that gives some shade to this neglected piece of Devon.

" It's going to be alright, we can sort it out", I mutter to myself.

I continue with the inspection of my new home, as I walk quietly around the garden and turn back to survey my new abode. Christ, it really must be the ugliest caravan in the world! A square box on wheels, no shape to the walls, no style and with the strangest of bowed roofs.

It actually reminds me of a photograph I have, taken possibly by me or my father, on a caravan holiday in Wales. I would have been about eleven. I can date it fairly accurately, because my sister is sitting naked in a small plastic washing up bowl, positioned on the grass in front of the caravan, being bathed by my mother in the sunshine. She must have been around six months old.

That was about 40 years ago, and my new home looks exactly like it. However, this ex-holiday caravan, (which has been used as a residence) is now going to be my permanent home.

Situated on a complex of mobile homes, yet not like a trailer park, typical in America. These retirement Parks, are for people who have reached the grand old age of fifty. People move from the city to have a quiet existence on this kind of complex. I guess. I feet ready for that.

It is indeed a very quiet location, apart from the birds singing, and some distant traffic noise. Suddenly, standing there, acutely aware of the wondrous sounds of nature, I realise that there is another sound, an intruder to nature, destroying the natural harmony. It's snoring! My eyes dart in the direction of the caravan to the left of me, on the adjacent plot, squinting hard to see it, through this jungle, my private garden.

And what a sight! Painted in the vilest, most horrible green with a white mid band, looking more like a builders' site hut than a mobile home. It is approximately ten feet away, through the undergrowth. The walls are actually vibrating! I smile, it's obviously my new neighbour, sleeping.

Male or female, I wonder?

The distinctive sound of the ubiquitous milk float breaks the moment. It buzzes and rattles to a stop at the top of my driveway. I walk towards it. The driver jumps out.

"Mornin' young sir, my name's John. Would you like me to drop by every morning?"

A little surprised by his happy tone, I reply,

 "Well yes, of course, John. My name's Norman."

"Norr-man, is it," in his Devon accent. "Pleased to meet you. On your own?"

"Yes, I am."

"Just the one pint, will it be then?"

"Better make it two, John," I say with a laugh. "My dog drinks a pint a day."

"Right you are then, young sir," he smiles.

"Big dog then?"

I say nothing, leaving him to wonder.

As I take the milk from him, a lady in her dressing gown walks down her drive and starts talking to John. I am curious. This is the first time I have seen her, in fact, I haven't seen anyone yet in my road. She is from the caravan next door on the right. Or should I be polite and call it a mobile home?

Her curtains had twitched a few times when I was looking at the place some weeks ago. But this is my first sight of her.

Our homes are separated by our two garages. They are hardly visible. Totally overgrown with blackberry bushes and shaded by tall pines. She is wearing a pink dressing gown; it reaches down to her ankles. She looks quite slender. A tall woman with long, bedraggled, grey hair. Her face is very pale, in her late sixties. She takes a single pint of milk from John and as she walks back up her drive, she looks towards me but doesn't acknowledge me. The first encounter. I have a feeling there will be more.

John moves his milk float to the end of the road, actually a cul-de-sac. He stops at the next group of property's. These homes are what you would call, 'mobile homes'. Purpose-built and more up to date, unlike mine and my immediate neighbours . We are all in the old original part of this *Retirement Park,* which now spreads over several acres, there are still some old vans in our section, each home having a garden plot, most of them well cared for.

I watch as John goes around the next few homes to see if I can get a glimpse of any more of the residents but no luck. I know there must be some interesting people here.

It won't be long before I get some of the guys who work for me to help with some demolition before I begin the refurbishment of this tired old place. We need some planning consent before we can proceed with the remodelling of the internal walls and change the outside appearance but the banging will soon begin. A skip is needed for the old doors and wall sections and that bloody awful brown carpet will have to go.

The quiet tranquil park and its residents will love me!

But I have come here to live not die.

Later that morning, I am back in the office. It is less than two miles away from the new place, it's mid-May and I am coming out of my winter blues period.

'Seasonal Affective Disorder.' I found out about this depression recently, they call it SAD. It's probably been the reason for many things I have done in my life that I could never explain.

My mind, is not on the workload of the day. I am actually watching the little tight rounded backside that belongs to our office cleaner. She's been cleaning the offices for about a year now. She is around forty and has a great personality. However, it's the first time I have really noticed the cute ass, currently on display, bending over my prized gramophone unit with a rag and the polish in her hands. I often play records while I am working. Old albums from my collection that with each house move over the years gets smaller, only retaining ones with special meaning.

I have a spring in my step today.

 "Would you like a brew, boss?"

I sit upright in my chair and with a little clearing of my throat and mind. (The rear of her, growing more attractive each second…having been on my own for a while).

"Yes, Julie that would be lovely," Although it isn't the first thing on my mind.

"Okay then, two sugars?"

Just then a delivery of timber arrives outside the workshop. Some of the plywood is for me, for the walls of my new home, so I go out to inspect and sign for it.

Back in my office, Julie brings in the tea.

"How's the new place coming on?" she asks.

I explain briefly.

"If you need a cleaner, you can call me."

She leaves the cup on the desk after adjusting the position of the handle to face me and bounces out of the office.

Full of fun, Julie liked a drink and smoked a joint. Her life up to that point had been eventful. She had left home in her teens, been a hippy and a traveller, going from town to town, festival to festival, working when and where she could, so a bit of a rebel and possibly a handful. Julie had also indicated that she would like to come to one of my local gigs that I had procured for the summer.

The phone rings and I am soon back into the routine of running the hire depot, one of three in a small group of companies, the Head Office based in Oxford. I have been there for four years and made a lot of friends in the area.

I relocated here with my girlfriend. We had been together for six years. She was eleven years younger than me and I loved her very much. However, tight finances and her two young children added towards the reasons which resulted in our recent breakup.

We met in Belgium, of all places at a Cliff Richard concert, on a very cold winter's evening. But I digress.

Before I continue and tell you about this period of my life, I want to take you right back to my childhood.

I was born in the city of Salford in the North of England, on the border with Manchester, in a hospital called 'Hope'. Good start!

I came into the world four years after my mother and father got married in 1946. They were living over a bakery. Dad was a sewing machine mechanic, my mother a seamstress. At the age of three we moved, literally just a few miles, to a little house close to Old Trafford, the home of the Manchester United Football Club. It was situated typically in a row of small back to back terraced houses. Matchstick men canvases, courtesy of LS Lowry. That was us.

 Imagine a hot summer's day, the air heavy with smog from the nearby factory chimneys. A small boy is playing, poking and flicking the melted tar from in between the street cobblestones, with a discarded wooden lollipop stick. That's me, happy days and innocent ones. No electronic gadgets then. The things you could make with lollipop sticks!

I remember one of the highlights of the week. The visit of the 'Rag & Bone man'. You would hear in the distance, the sound of steel-rimmed, rickety, wooden wheels, being distorted and twisted by the slightly irregular, rounded, unevenly-laid, granite cobbles in the road, followed by the clonk of a mule's feet, along with his cry. "Ragbon, ragbon," as the old tramp-looking Rag & Bone man approached. I must have been about five years old. Us kids would give him old clothes and unwanted household items, with the permission of our mothers. I guess, you could say, he was the recycling man of his day. He would give us, in return, depending on the amount of rubbish offered to him, a toy, especially if there was a bit of metal amongst the load. Or, if Mother insisted, a 'donkey stone'.

Donkey stones were used to clean your front step. It left the sandstone steps looking a natural colour. We didn't have much in the fifties 'up north', but what we did have we were proud of.

 Incidentally, "What do you call a donkey with three legs?" 'Wonky.'

I recently discovered my Great Grandad, whom I never knew about until recently, used to deliver coal with a horse and cart, from his home in Hankey Park, Salford my home town.

I was not a healthy child. I had respiratory problems, asthma. Most of my early years were spent in bed at home in our little two up two down house in Salford. My bedroom was at the back of the house, directly off a very steep staircase rising from the kitchen, compacted into the smallest space possible. The veritable Harry Potter scenario. It would not meet health and safety regulations today. These stairs had a small landing at the top leading to both mine and my parents room. No bathroom. All we had was an outside WC at the bottom of the yard, a thunder box.

During the night, if you needed the toilet, we wouldn't go outside, unless it was a big job! Instead we would use a ceramic pot that looked like a German war helmet. We called it a 'Gerry'. It was kept under the bed.

There is a well-known saying if you're very poor. 'We don't have a pot to piss in.' That's where it comes from, I reckon.

If you wanted to have a bath, you would have to wait until Friday, unless it was your birthday. Each and every Friday, the galvanised tin bath would come indoors, lifted from its position hanging on a large nail on a wall in the back yard.

It would be positioned, ready for filling, in front of a coal fire, glowing in the old cast iron range in the kitchen. This was originally used for all the cooking, pre-war. The water to fill the bath would cascade from a thin tube attached to the gas heater over the sink, 'The Geezer'. It had a spout long enough to swing out into the bath. Dad first, then Mum then me, the same water for all of us. Happy days!

My tiny bedroom was cold and draughty. It had a high ceiling and a large sash window, with paper-thin glass, which would rattle with the wind and let in the cold air. The only heating was from the coal fire down in the kitchen, that would drift up the stairs. I spent many long days in bed; my mother would sometimes be out working, part-time in the factory in the next street, so she could pop in and out to keep an eye on me, or she would be busy downstairs. My father would be at work, doing long hours in a clothing factory. But I wasn't lonely. I had a great friend in the corner of my room. A very old valve radio, from the twenties, maybe.

It was basically a wooden box, re-varnished and refurbished by my father. It was about two feet high and around fourteen inches square. The shape of the fretwork which covered the speaker, the tuning dial and the position of the knobs for the volume etc. were arranged in such a way, it gave the impression, to me, of a little smiling face.

What joy! I enjoyed hours and hours of music every day, soaking into my brain.

There was swing, jazz, from popular big bands of the day, American and English, plus classical music with some occasional new sounds, like *Skiffle*. The start of rock and roll.

I also loved listening to fantastically narrated stories, taking me to places I would never know, or see, or so I thought.

One of my sharpest memories is that of the lunchtime specials most weekdays. The broadcasts would come live from factory canteens around the country. It was a way of boosting industry after the war years. It was called '*Workers Playtime*'.

Featured on a regular basis were artists such as Peter Sellers, Tony Hancock, Anne Shelton, Julie Andrews, Morecambe and Wise, and three people that later in life I would briefly work with, Terry Thomas, Ronnie Hilton and Bob Monkhouse.

 Another show I enjoyed was '*Music while you work*'.

This was again aimed at keeping workers happy while having their lunch. This programme consisted of live music from light orchestras, dance bands, brass bands and instrumental ensembles. A variety of music filled my ears, from all genres.

When I was well enough to go to school it was not the normal everyday infant affair. My school was classed as an open-air school, for kids with health problems, like TB and my problem, asthma.

Most days we would have to spend at least an hour sleeping outside under a canopy on a fold-away bed with a coarse, heavy, woolly blanket over us, winter and summer. Education was secondary to health, which did not help my three Rs. I do have a vague memory of going to another local school for a period, it may have been only weeks, I don't know. My memory is very vague but I do remember rows of tiered desks, rising, either side of the room, maybe five different levels.

The old desks were covered with lots of names engraved deep in the wood and badly stained with ink, spilled from the ceramic inkwells, at the side of each desktop that would open to reveal even more facts about pupils' pasts. The inkwells are now sadly dry. We used individual small black slate boards and white chalk as well.

 I can also envisage the outside yard and remember playing with old car tyres, rolling them around the walled play area.

'Ordsall Board School' was a huge Victorian building, severely damaged after the second World War and left to rot in the late sixties, as the whole area was cleared of its rows of back to back houses.

They called it slum clearance; I believe they're in the process of doing it again now after building cheap concrete, ugly, unhealthy high-rise flats, which became an urban jungle.

Alan Clarke and *Graham Nash* also went to Ordsall School and went on to form *The Hollies* and *Eddie Coleman*. 'A Busby Babe', one of the young football players for Manchester United, who sadly died in the Munich Air crash of 1958, was also a pupil, although a few years before I was there.

Eventually, when I was a little older, around seven I guess, the family moved into a new home on a new council estate out of the city, closer to the countryside where the air was good. Apparently.

I was then at a normal Junior school, but my education level was below most pupils in my year. However, I gained a lot of confidence there. I was still having periods of ill health and having to be away from my classes. Music again was my saviour, and I was now the proud owner of a small record player and an expanding record collection. We also acquired a television. Black and white of course.

I also loved to draw and had a plethora of coloured pencils, developing a skill for landscapes and I would create scenes from the stories off the radio, that had been created in my head.

By the age of seven, I had also had two girlfriends, Barbara and Denise. The memory of playing doctors and nurses comes back to me shamefully.

The blueprint for the rest of my life is right there. Back in the first years of my young life. *Music, women and radio.*

At the age of eleven, unfortunately for me, we moved again to a new district, leaving my young, new-found friends behind. It was only twenty miles away but back then it seemed more like hundreds. I never settled at my new education establishment. I was an alien, my accent was different, this area had a different dialect and the majority of the boys had moved up to the secondary school together and were all pals. I was also singled out because I couldn't play football or athletics because of my asthma. I resented that so much. There were days when I just went down the driveway and hid in my father's garage until home time.

I gradually lost any confidence I had regained over the last few years.

It was almost four years of hell, other than a few practical classes that I enjoyed in the last year and a musically-minded older boy who became my friend that played piano. Robert, I think was his name. Together we tried to write a few songs, using lyrics that I had already started to compose. One song was called *'Summer Love'*, about a girl I'd met during the long sunny days of our school holiday.

I couldn't wait for the weekends. I would sit and listen to the radio. Sundays were especially important, as the week's top-selling records would be played. '*The Top 20,*' on the BBC was an exciting, informative couple of hours with Allan Freeman, known as Fluff who sadly passed away recently. I had now been blessed with the latest technology, a reel to reel tape recorder, a combined Christmas/birthday present. With this new machine I was now able to record songs from the radio and record myself, singing over recently-broadcast popular songs, even the latest single of the week.

I wanted to be part of this fantastic music industry that was exploding around the world, encouraged by local bands like *The Beatles, The Searchers, The Mindbenders*. They called this 'The Merseysound.' It was happening just a few miles down the road in Liverpool. Then there was *Billy Fury,* also from Liverpool, and the capital, London, was giving us *Tommy Steel, Adam Faith, Cliff Richard* and a host of American singers. Rock and roll had arrived.

I knew I could be like them. My parents didn't understand this new musical era. I understand that now, as I have grown older and find that some modern songs sound like utter rubbish to me, just as the songs I enjoyed then, did to my parents. Back then, for one reason or another, they could not and did not know how to guide me. I wanted to learn how to play the piano, but sadly never got the chance. My biggest regret.

The last year at school I worked hard, after finding something I was good at. I enjoyed technical drawing and art, and this was where I excelled. I got extra tuition on these subjects and it separated me from the lower grade, trouble makers, and riff raff in my normal class.

I also knew it would help me find a job doing something I liked, never for a moment daring to believe that I could be part of the music business.

If using the right side of my brain was okay, the left (the academic) was not quite up there. My Maths and English uneasy to grasp.

Again, I had little guidance from my school or my parents on how to develop or improve on this. So with this positive period of art and technical tutorial behind me, in my final year, I left school with these words from my technical tutor embedded in my head, after I told him I wanted to work in a drawing office.

 " Lad you will ncvcr qualify as a draughtsman." The bastard.

With those words of encouragement ringing in my head! I was determined to succeed and it wasn't long before I was applying for jobs, anywhere, everywhere, even a jewellers in the city.

I pumped petrol in a garage, stacked shelves in a supermarket and eventually, I was accepted as a clerk in an office at a large steel works in Trafford Park. It was a start.

This company also had a large drawing office and I would have the chance to move up to that department at a later date. They sent me to Salford college to take my exams in Building Construction. There I met some great young guys. It was so good to be among like-minded people who I thought liked me.

Trafford Park was and still is a complex of factories and warehouses, that grew from the Industrial revolution and the success of the nearby docks, which is now where the BBC's Media city is located.

I would have to catch two buses to work. It would take an hour on average to get there. Every town in the greater Manchester area had direct bus routes to Trafford Park, the main centre of industry.

Convoys of buses, cars, motorbikes, and cycles crossed the giant mechanical iron, road swing bridges that connected and, allowed access to this industrial area, encircled by the *Manchester Ship Canal.* Thousands, no armies of people would cram onto the main two through roads, zigzagging in front of the buses, trying to avoid the hundreds of railway lines that crossed these roads and avenues. These railway lines connected the factories directly to the nearby docks. I said avenues because this was how the roads in the central area, were named. First Avenue, Second Avenue, etc. Obviously influenced by the Americans, and yes, there were some large American companies there, like Westinghouse.

I vividly remember cold, wet mornings; it would still be dark when arriving at the offices.

 I would enter via the main doors, pass through a reception area, past the MD's office, into a central corridor in this Victorian workhouse. The corridor had offices either side, the walls constructed with solid wooden panels to waist height and, glass windows above. Allowing visibility, nobody could avoid being watched by the bosses.

It had its advantages! If I was in the office before the girls in the typing pool came in, I could enjoy the view of them changing out of their wet clothes and stockings. The comptometer girls had an office directly adjacent to my window, several whom were stunning would hoic their skirts up above the knee, put their feet up on their chairs, remove their nylons, dry their legs. Pressed up behind the filing cabinets and on the cusp of being sixteen, this was a very erotic experience.

One of my workmates and mentor at this time, John Virgo, became a world champion snooker player and TV presenter. He was five or six years older than me and good fun. His outbursts of impressions, Roy Orbison, especially, during tea breaks were delightful.

We would go for a pint and play snooker most lunchtimes and return to work via the bookmakers, good training for me, being so young. He opened my eyes in more ways than one, so did, the sexy glossy magazines I kept discovering hidden in the toilet block, with the occasional pages stuck together for some reason. Pints of beer in the pub with John Virgo. His lessons about women and our talks about music fired up my desire to pursue singing even more. One of our conversations included a guy from the drawing office, Paul, his last name escapes me. He played guitar and had recently left a local band, I forget why. But it happens all the time - people fall out and get jealous. I too know that now. Anyway, it seems that shortly after he exited the line-up, they had a record in the charts. The band was *Herman's Hermits.*

After a year of buses, I bought myself a brand new motorbike on the never-never. This gave me total freedom, to go anywhere whenever I wanted. I even took the six-foot something John Virgo to some of his first big snooker matches in and around Manchester. Just imagine him perched on the back of a little Honda 50, complete with cue in hand.

I did eventually move into the drawing office and almost managed to start a relationship with one of the older comptometer girls. I frequently sat on the bus with her, travelling home after work. She was possibly five years older than me and if I hadn't got my motorbike to commute I think I would have had a chance. But it wouldn't be long before I was in an interesting relationship.

A comptometer, by the way, was an adding machine, as big as a desk.

The world was changing fast. The year was now 1964. I was happy, away from that fucking awful school. I was writing a song a day, during my tea breaks. The tunes stored in my brain, the lyrics flooding into my head, written on bits of scrap paper, with little dots and squiggles above the words reminding me of how the tunes went. No other person in the world would understand such shorthand.

They were short pop songs, typical of the day, the vast majority never to be heard but some would be recorded a few years down the line.

'One fine day', would be the first.

On a very wet night, in torrential rain, on the way home from work, over some of those railway lines I spoke about, my bike skidded over on its side, almost ending up under an oncoming train! Thankfully, I bounced on my arse in the opposite direction. Apart from my pride, no bones broken, but with the bike out of action, I was back on the bus.

Desperate to find a way to put my vocal talents to use, I searched the adverts in the local paper, and at weekends and would look on the notice boards at the music shops in downtown Manchester. I had for many years, probably from being twelve years old, regularly gone to Manchester and visited the electrical junk shops and music shops, looking at everything relating to making music. London Road on the south side, had several old rickety wooden-cladded junk shops standing on their own, surrounded by wasteland used for parking. I guess the open space was left after the bombing in the Second World War. Nowadays it is a huge junction for the city bypass. Anyway, those dirty cluttered premises specialised in selling items for the DIY electrician, model makers, etc, and sold a wide variety of old radio equipment and record players. Aladdin's cave to me.

Each week I would buy something and fund my trip with pocket money earned from delivering groceries for the local shop, on an old black bicycle with a large basket at the front. Don't ask me how many eggs I broke. Sometimes, I would slip a packet of cigarettes in my pocket from behind the counter and sell them at school.

I bought several types of radio speakers in those junk shops, from ten bob to a couple of pounds. Some were oval, some square, as well as normal round ones, all of different dimensions and I wired them up to my *Dansette* auto-change record player. I was experimenting with sound; stereo systems or surround sound were a thing of the future. So I suppose I was actually developing my own, with wires tucked under the carpets around my mother's front room.

I fondly remember one particular Saturday morning in Manchester, around fourteen, I was looking in the window of one of those electrical bazaars and spotted a microphone! Placed among bits of second hand parts at the back of the window display, it nestled in its box, caressed by blue velvet. It was a *Reslo,* made in America. It was shouting, "I am yours."

I just had to have it. Absolutely gorgeous, with a highly polished steel finish. Today, it is classed as retro and a collector's item.

 I think it was probably about £25, I can't remember exactly. I placed a deposit on it and each week thereafter, I paid some more until it was mine. All I had to do then was put it to good use!

 I continued to read the notice boards and classifieds, hoping to see an opportunity for me. Eventually, it paid off. A local guitarist was advertising to form a band. I contacted him and we got on like a house on fire. He played well for his age and he sang. Norman was his name (yes, that's right), seventeen, a year older than me and he lived less than ten minutes away. We practised for several months and The *Normans Duo* was born.

I then contacted a number of booking agents and we started attending weekend auditions for the Federation of Club secretaries. These guys, the federation chaps, were no more than jumped-up little assholes, booking acts into their relevant working men's clubs or political associations. I didn't know that then. It took me a few years to discover, through experience, in the beginning I thought they were god's. Give the average working man a little power and they abuse it. *Clubland* was full of them.

Singers, musicians, in fact, any performer worth his salt, aspired to be professional, even if they were only semi-professional, as most of them were. They, the assholes, were far from it. There are lots of jokes and stories about these guys. This one is mine, from a period later in my career.

I am in the dressing room. I have had the briefing with the two musicians at the club. Keyboard player and drummer, both young guys, were very competent. We had gone through my sheet music, most of it specially written for me, in my style. They are now on stage playing some great tunes, building the atmosphere. I am preparing for my big entrance, the guys finish their set, the concert secretary grabs the microphone. He then, in typical fashion, blows down it, something you should never do, to make sure it is on. "Testing, testing," emits from his mouth, followed by, my introduction? No, followed by, "Ladies and gentlemen, Audrey Williams died today... two minutes' silence please."

After the deadly silence and without any introduction, he just says my name! And we launch into a very up-tempo song as planned, (Very embarrassing). Follow that, as they say!

It's true about the old stories when the say the singer was stopped in the middle of a song because the pies had arrived or the bingo tickets were on sale.

My Dad, bless him, took us to our gigs in his Austin A40. We were earning £5 a show. Back then my weekly wage at the office was around £6, so we were in the money.

Our gear was very basic, except for that very expensive microphone, the one I had bought some years before.

My Dad is still my biggest fan and at the time of writing this, he is ninety-two.

The gigs turned out to be good for me, I started learning how to handle people, including the 'assholes,' and the applause was good for the soul. We got lots of return bookings, so I reckon we did our job well. We sang the songs from the charts. It was 1964.

We could not go wrong for material, as the best songs, to this day, were being released in their hundreds then. We were thirty miles away if that, from Liverpool, so we rehearsed Beatles songs and releases from other bands from Liverpool, like Gerry and Pacemakers, The Searchers, also Manchester based, Hollies, and of course, Elvis. It was a very exciting time for me. At last, I was doing what I had always dreamed of.

The song *Summer Love* that I wrote while at school, was never recorded but I remember some of the lyrics.

Summer love only a summer love,

that drifted into the fall.

Could this mean that summer love,

won't be ending at all?

Our love is so true it will last through summer

and into the fall,

Wait for my summer call and I'll be there.

Chapter 2

A Decade of Discovery

I got my motorbike back after the accident and started doing some trips out each night. The telephonist at work, Anne, said she used to go dancing in Eccles, a nearby town, before she had a bad accident herself. She had been hit by a car and her legs had been badly broken, so her mobility was limited. Her job, to connect all the telephones to the different departments, could be done from a seated position, ideal for her. She was happy go lucky. I stopped and chatted with her every time I passed by her small room.

 I was asking her for advice regarding women, when she told me about the dance academy. "A good place to meet people," she explained with a wink.

Coincidentally, one of the guys in the drawing office, Ian, who I was at college with, went there. He was slightly older than I was. So I arranged to meet him on a Sunday, a teaching day. I arrived on my bike and parked up, removed my helmet and overtrousers, before climbing the stairs up to the Court School of Dance, adjusting myself and checking my image in the many mirrors.

It was above the local cinema. At the top of a wide ornate staircase was the foyer with double doors leading to the dance hall. The place was buzzing, a mixture of girls and boys of all ages having tuition.

I spotted Ian in the far corner. Not difficult to locate at six foot something. He was standing with another guy in his late teens, so I crossed over to join them. This meeting would form a lasting relationship, to this day with the other guy, also called Ian. I was introduced to a slim lady with blond hair in her forties. Around five feet tall, yet with high heels, she was able to look me directly in the eye. She was the principal teacher. I signed up and within a week was attending classes.

I thought dancing could pay dividends, I wanted to be on stage, maybe even get into musicals. It had the other advantage like getting close to the opposite sex, sometimes extremely close. You could touch, feel, hold many shapes and sizes of the female form. It was also great fun and of course we did it all to great music.

After several weeks I was able to waltz, jive, quickstep and was learning latino dancing. I regularly went to my new friends flat on a Saturday afternoon. Ian's mum would prepare some food for us before we went dancing. He played acoustic guitar. I had learned a few chords, myself, so we played and listened to some records, before his mum served up some grub.

Saturday night was a social night, with a disco atmosphere. We danced and flirted with a lot of girls, in-between drinking an espresso and consuming a doughnut. I am just comparing then, with the way kids socialise now. What went wrong?

Young Ian was actually involved with one of the young dance tutors. He was good looking and went to a private school. He had loads of confidence for his age. I think her name was Jean. She was a year or so older than the two of us. I got introduced to her older sister, Sheila, also a teacher, only by a year to eighteen months older than her sister, but that age gap put her at least three years older than me.

I didn't complain - I was taught how to dance, wasn't I?

Needless to say, we were having a great time of it. As months passed Ian was still going with Jean. Shelia, however, had moved on to her next victim. I didn't mind actually, as I had met a young girl at an Aprils Fool's dance, my wife to be. Crazy, it was less than two years since I had left school and there I was thinking about getting engaged! I was still green, but thought I knew everything! After a few weeks, I introduced her to my parents, as you do.

She was a Catholic girl with Irish parents, the eldest of 5, two sisters and two brothers. Desperate for someplace to be alone, I said we would babysit my little sister for my parents, so they could enjoy a night out. They hadn't had many recently because of my new-found activities. They agreed and went out for the night. My sister, about three years old, fourteen years younger than me, was asleep. I was alone with my new girlfriend for the first time. She was very petite, under five feet tall, slender, long brown hair. She wore a light blue silk dress, a little old-fashioned, I thought but money was tight then.

We were both nervous about being alone. We never disclosed if this was our first time, as we awkwardly did what came naturally.

This was love. Or was it?

I had nothing to compare it to. We both knew nothing except that we were having lots of fun.

For the next three years we saw each other almost every night, weekdays usually at her parent's house with our feet up against the dining room door! In the summer, we would find secluded places and play in the back of my Mini - my first car. Marriage was the natural next step..

We were kids doing what their parents had done before them. We became parents, too. Too quickly, too early in life.

I also severed my relationship with Norman shortly after discovering sex. My courtship was more important, or so it seemed.

We were married on a tight budget on April 4, 1970, as near as damn it, six years from our first meeting, on April Fool's night.

After a year in a rented flat, where our first child Karen was born, we bought a new house, around the spring of 1972. The paint was still wet the day we moved in. A terraced property, two bedrooms, gardens front and rear plus a garage. All this for £3,100. Sounds cheap, but I had to forge the mortgage application by adding a '1', in front of my yearly salary to get the loan.

I was making more money at the weekends, working the clubs with a new partner who played guitar, than I was at my daytime job, but what the taxman didn't know...

Jim, my new guitar man, worked in the same office. I had moved on from Trafford park, having been made redundant.

I got a job as a design draughtsman for industrial heating systems, mostly fuelled by cheap diesel oil. Having had a year in the drawing office in Trafford park, at the steel works, plus a certificate from college, I was able to bluff my way into the job. One day, shortly after starting, I was sent to do a survey at a factory some two hundred miles away, having just passed my driving test. I came back, not only with the design for the system, but also a contract to proceed and full payment, worth several thousand pounds. I was given a company car and my job progressed to another level.

Jim and I practised at night and sometimes in the office, polishing up our vocals, eventually producing fine harmonies with some visual routines, that lent themselves to doing cabaret.

We were out three nights a week, working some big clubs, The Poco la Poco, The Cumberland, The Talk of the North, working alongside, Bob Monkhouse, The Grumbleweeds, and The American Drifters.

Sadly for Jim, it got too much for him. He wanted to study and he had recently married. I was his best man and he was mine, a new baby and the job got in the way.

Our directors put a lot of trust in us; it paid off for them. We got results, but actually I achieved my sales targets easily. It was a boom time, until the global oil crisis hit.

I had four great years, a wage upgrade, a bigger car each year, including a Ford Mexico and the use of the boss's Jaguar. I also had two trips to our manufacturers in Denmark in a private plane' my first time in an aeroplane. One return journey I shared the cockpit and flew the five seater, Cessna, over the North Sea.

Times were changing, I had to keep focused. Higher fuel prices could mean no sales, so I started looking at other opportunities, the job section in the national papers as well as The Stage/Variety papers.

One Sunday morning I was enjoying a read and a Sunday cuppa in bed. *Positioned* against the large bedroom window the morning sun was streaming in. A stone hit the glass and I heard a voice, calling me. I opened the window to see my neighbour and actually in a way an agent of mine. He shouted up to me from the centre of my lawn,

"Norm, you'll never believe it, I've won the pools, (similar to the lottery), a million quid!"

"Fuck off, Danny, don't wind me up on a Sunday morning," I replied. He always was a bit of a joker.

"No. It's true," he said as he walked away, disappointed by my reaction. I closed the window.

Amazingly he had been telling the truth and I was the first person, apart from his wife, he had told.

Danny was then, by an input of funds, made a partner in the booking agency that created most of my singing work at that time. I was working solo and he used to call me his Sinatra. Months later his daughter was kidnapped for a ransom and shortly after that the whole family went to Benidorm to live. That was the last I ever saw of him.

I heard he had set up an agency there but I never got the chance to talk to him again. The kid was returned unharmed by the way.

Our second child was born in the new house in 1972. At twenty-three years old and another mouth to feed, I had to make more money. I was spending it faster than I was making it.

It wasn't all going on running the home. I was clubbing several times a month, in some of the most salubrious clubs in Cheshire. Places like *Bredbury Hall,* frequented by footballers and highflyers and *Foo Foo's Palace* in Manchester, that had some low flyers, as I remember. I was living it up with two guys who played music and wrote songs, plus ran an entertainment agency. Mr 10% and his mate. One of them disappeared to Spain overnight, never to be seen again after a dodgy business scam.

The famous *Strawberry Studios,* the home of 10cc, was located just streets away from their home and office. It seemed worth a chance to hang out with them, you never know. The music business is all about being in the right place at the right time. An old cliché but true, *'Strawberry'* was the only recording studio outside London when it opened in 1967. Then named Intercity Studios.

We fooled around with women during this crazy time, but things were good at home, so I was being faithful, my focus purely on getting a music break, using any opportunity. I wanted to achieve something, make my family secure.

Money was an important factor in this game of life and although you could make money from the music business, once established, a decent day job was a must. I was trawling through the tabloids as usual when I saw an opportunity The advertisement was worded:

Consultant wanted for a National Energy Conservation Company. Perfect, the next big thing, hopefully. Expensive oil... *Insulate....* They were manufacturing, new construction systems, it was an American company.

I was interviewed in Yorkshire at one of their factories. Bingo! I got the job, of course! I knew how to handle people by then. I was full of bullshit-confidence and I could sell myself.

 I was soon heading down south to the county of Kent, to the HQ for induction.

It was an area of the country new to me, in fact, I had not really spent any time in the south of England except for holidays, in Devon as a youth.

I was introduced to management and production staff. The people were very nice, a different culture down there, people who seemed to have different standards. I don't know why. Maybe they were better educated because it was near the capital. I felt like I was finally moving up the social ladder. Important introductions over, I had a meeting with the personnel officer to get all my details down on their system. I was escorted to the office. I knocked on the door and waited and a female voice answered.

" Come in."

On my best behaviour, I had to make a good first impression with absolutely everyone I met today. (You never know what's around the corner)

Imagine the scene, if you can. Me wearing a new suit, a black and white herringbone design, double breasted, with a slight flair to the trousers, my hair fair in colour, shoulder length, the style then, slightly curly at the shoulder, blow-dried and well groomed. I had a very neat poncho style moustache, and a large pair of spectacles, accentuating my light blue eyes, with a clear almost white frame, all the fashion. My shoes, actually boots, were high-heeled, again the norm then. I was walking tall.

I took a deep breath, not the first time that day, before entering. My wide smile stretched even wider when I clapped eyes on her.

 Oh, by the way, guess what time of year it was? May. I had been feeling very happy for the last few weeks, emerging from the SAD syndrome again.

She glanced at me briefly before diverting her eyes back to some paperwork on her desk.

"Sit down please, I will just be a moment."

I sat in a chair a little distance from her desk. I settled myself and adjusted my tie, looking around the office, moving my eyes rather than my head and soon focused on her legs. From my seated position I had a perfect view of them, long, very long and slender.

Nice, I thought, very nice. I was at this point, slightly slumping down in my chair to see as much as I could. Mini skirts were in fashion. I got an eyeful. I was deep in thought when she said.

"Hello, how are you? Welcome to the company. My name is Angela."

"Hello, I'm good and I'm having an interesting day, thanks."

As well as long legs she had long blonde hair, fair skin, a nice face, not stunning, waring little makeup, except for some deep red lipstick. I am a sucker for red lipstick.

She sat upright, in her chair and took a good look at me, I adjusted my slightly relaxed posture, trying not to give away the fact that I was transfixed by her inviting legs. Our eyes met.

"You're from Manchester?"

"Yes, that's right."

I am now staring at her cleavage, her breasts ready to burst through a gap in her white blouse.

"I need to go through some details with you. Do you have your driving license and tax details?"

She smiled as I reached across to her, handing her the documents. We continued to go through the form filling, my eyes now firmly fixed on her face. Well, it was only polite!

She was well-spoken with a good position in the company; I was won over by the local Kent accent. I had only seen and heard women like this on television, I was fascinated.

We seemed to get on very well. Angela made me feel relaxed and we both smiled a lot and laughed as we got to know each other. She explained that there were two other people starting today and we would all be staying the night at a hotel a few miles away.

"Your new company car is waiting for you there. Here are the keys, It's an orange Marina." (*An Austin Morris classic!*).

"Thank you, I am sure I will put it to good use," thinking about travelling to my gigs!

"I will come up tonight to make sure everything is okay."

"I am looking forward to it," I said, or something like that.

"See you tonight."

She stood up, opened the door for me, then pointed the way back to the main office. As we passed in the doorway, she reached for my hand, as you naturally would and, I got the feeling it could turn out to be an interesting night.

I met the other two guys in the main sales office and after a brief introduction, we were driven to the hotel. We got there around 5.30pm. It was a pleasant evening. It's warmer here down south, I thought.

I took full advantage of the bathroom facilities in this modern hotel, changed into some casual clothes and met the guys in the garden, we celebrated our new jobs with a cold beer. We got to know more about each other. I was working the Lancashire area, the other guys Yorkshire and the Midlands. As we chatted, a blue, open-top sports car pulled into the car park. It was her.

"I'm on expenses," she said. "What are you guys drinking?" As she passed us swiftly with such a confident stride, I could swear she flicked her hair back, marking her dominance. We followed her to the bar, like sheep. After a few drinks we were all getting on fine. We relocated to the restaurant to eat and washed it down with wine.

 I guess it was around 10pm when we finished. It had been a long day, as we had all travelled by train from our homes early that morning. Mike, the guy from Yorkshire on the six-fifteen from Leeds, my departure time a little more forgiving, just after eight. We also had to drive back to our own locations early in the morning as well, so the boys said their farewells and headed back to their rooms, leaving Angela and myself alone.

"Angela, do you have far to drive?" I asked.

"Drive, no! I knew I would have a drink tonight and I am here to look after you guys, so I booked a room here for the night. Fancy a night cap?"

"Hell yes."

We didn't have any kind of body contact at that point. We sat very close together though for the night cap. There was no indication of what was going to happen next.

"Would you like to come up to my room, for a drink?"

A little stunned, I replied "Yes " Without a second thought.

I wasn't expecting that. I had been, I suppose, flirting with her most of the night, innocently!

We entered her room. I walked across to the window, not knowing how to handle the situation.

"What are you doing?"

"Just admiring the view and looking at my new car,"

"It's warm tonight, open the window, would you please?"

 We talked for a long time. The room was at half-light and a slight breeze was drifting through, the sound of the traffic on the A2, the only things invading our privacy. As I listened to her, I couldn't help wondering if all the women were like that down south. It was the early seventies. The swinging sixties had just changed our attitudes to relationships and I often thought that we were a little behind the times, up north.

She told me she was married to a guy who worked for a paint manufacturer, he was often away working at a factory in Blackburn.

"It's been two years since we married. It's not the same now we've have grown apart. I think I am too young for him." Indicating he was older. It also seemed that her mother did not like him, nor his family.

She knew all about me of course, after taking my details, for the company files, so no secrets, she knew I was married.

I was looking at her in the soft light of the hotel room, as we sat on the bed, relaxed after the consumption of a fair amount of alcohol. God her legs were long! She turned her back to me, took off her cotton blouse and said "Unclip my bra," I hesitated then fumbled with the clasp. She just laughed as her breasts dropped into my hands.

We joined the other new sales guys at the breakfast table the following morning. I looked across the table at her. She had a glow about her. Would the other guys suspect?

I just couldn't predict, as I drove home that day, how quickly the next twenty- four months would fly by and indeed how complicated my life would become.

Three weeks had passed since my trip to Head Office and my night with Angela. We had spoken on the telephone, regarding paperwork for the taxman and the usual documents required and as day's passed the conversations became more frequent and less official.

 This was before the days of mobile phones, so I would find myself in telephone boxes en route to a client, or at home I would wait for a convenient time to contact her. Sometimes I would hide behind the sofa, the expandable cable, of the *Trimphone* stretched as far as possible. The sofa would act as a sound barrier for the conversation, which would usually take place while my wife was in the bath.

I arranged to meet her during one of those secret, dubious conversations at Newport Pagnell Services, on the busy M1 where there was a motel. We booked in around midday for an afternoon of sex. What else?

We closed the door after hanging the 'Do Not Disturb' sign on the door handle and surfaced the following day, hungry as hell!

After a great British motorway services breakfast, we decided to take her car and go out for the day. The fact that I should be working hard at my new job, didn't enter my head. I was driving an open-topped MG sports car through the stunning Northamptonshire countryside with a sexy blonde, with the longest legs by my side, full of confidence in myself and my lovemaking. How much better could it get? We had a wonderful morning. I had never smiled so much! We visited a stately home, then stopped at a country pub. A real pub! Full of ambience, old oak-beamed ceilings, unchanged I would think for a couple of centuries.

The diamond-leaded patterned windows were open, letting the sun and warm breeze in, an allowing the smell of stale beer and nicotine out. Music was coming from a jukebox, possibly the only new addition to the establishment in recent times.

The voice of an angel filled the room. I was already feeling light-headed. I was in a romantic state of mind, so the lyrics I could hear really hit home.

"Loving you is easy because you're beautiful and everything I do is out of loving you."

These words from an unknown female singer with a fabulous angelic voice, lodged clearly in my mind. In the song you could hear the sound of birds singing. It was the perfect moment. We sat and listened and gazed into each other's eyes.

 But time ran out on our romantic adventure. We had to make our way back to the M1, retrieve my car and say our goodbyes.

It was a long journey back to Manchester. I stopped a while, called home and, gathered my thoughts before the reality of getting home to my family.

I parked up on my drive, took a deep breath before walking into the kitchen.

 "My God!" she said, "Where you have been?"

Immediately I felt guilty.

"Look at you," she said, "you're brown as a berry."

Driving the open-topped car today had exposed me to the sun. Add the wind factor as we sped along, the combination resulted in my face and neck tanning my usually pale skin.

"Thought you were working hard?" she laughed.

 I had a bath and changed, then returned and had my evening meal. After eating I was hesitant in preparing to go to bed. We talked for a while about my trip, I gave a good account of my *"business trip"* before we turned off the light and did what married people do.

Over the next few weeks I knuckled down, and surprisingly the new job was going well, as was the relationship with my wife, with a new vitality in the bedroom, and I have to say I was feeling on top of the world. The song I heard in the bar that day was being played every day on the radio. *Mini Ripperton* was the singer.

The song was called '*Loving you*'. Every time I heard it, it took me back to that moment and it still does.

At work I was using my artistic talents to make a film for the company. I bluffed my way into convincing them I could do it. I was on location, documenting the installation of a new product to be used in the construction of houses. I was in Hull, in the North of England, the wind blowing in from the North Sea. It had been a sunny day, good for filming but the wind left me feeling cold.

We finished late in the afternoon and fortunately I had an overnight stop at a hotel close by.

I was looking forward to a hot bath and a beer. I was just relaxing in the bath when there was a knock on the door, and the door opened.

"I am in the bath," I shouted, thinking it was the chambermaid.

"Good," was the reply. "I will join you."

I said, "Angela is that you?"

Seconds later she appeared wearing only a grin.

"Let me wash your back."

"Why are you here?" I asked.

"Well, I was asked to book your hotel for you last week, and today I had to go to Howden Works to do some personnel work, so here I am."

"This is a fantastic surprise," I said, "I have been thinking about you constantly."

"Nice surprise?" as she climbed into the bath.

"Yes, you bet," I said, turning the hot water tap on.

"I have another surprise for you. I'm moving to Manchester; I have a new job."

These lyrics are to a song that expresses my feelings about this relationship at this time.

'What are you doing to me?'

Hey what are you doing to me, I only see you now and again

But I'm in love with you, hey what are you doing to me

My head is spinning around and around, Yes I'm in love with you

Only twice we met but I know I will never forget

The day you told me, that you loved me

It was only an ordinary day and now I can't get you out of my mind.

This would become the B-side of my first single. **'One fine day'**.

Chapter 3

Something had to give

My job was great, no pressure or impossible deadlines. More of a consultant than a salesperson, sales targets didn't exist and the factory was busy. All good. My other colleague, Mike, based in the Yorkshire area, was also doing okay. Divorced, in his forties, living with his girlfriend, a beautiful 35 year old ex-model.

 After visiting the factory one particular day, I stayed over at their place in Bradford. Where I was introduced to something going by the name of chilli con carne. Later that evening I was invited into another room, to my surprise his girl, heavily pregnant, I may add, was standing in the corner of a large bay window. A light coloured silk cloth forming a backdrop filtered the light. Mike and I were now squatting on the floor in front of her while she posed, stark naked with child for his mate, a professional photographer. Stunning, totally breathtaking, a goddess. Mike had wanted to capture the moment. How lucky was I? Talk about being in the right place at the right time! Her breasts, naturally beautiful, had been skilfully enhanced with makeup by her friend, standing quietly in the shadows. There was a relaxed, albeit surreal feel in the air, although if truth be told, I was not quite as relaxed as I seemed.

I had never mixed with people like this; they had come through, sorry, lived through the sixties. That old familiar friend, inadequacy, was creeping in again.

The strange, oversized-looking cigarette being passed around seemed to be helping. Not a hard core smoker, just the occasional cigar, it didn't take more than a few seconds to realise what was cracking off. I accepted once and then a second time, dragging deeply, inhaling as much and for as long as I could, following it immediately with a gulp of red wine.

As the night went on, the more relaxed I became, a feeling of life in slow motion with a distant murmuring soundtrack, I told Mike and his beautiful partner about my recent turn of events. I was expecting to hear words of condemnation but they just took it all in, not once judging me, simply expressing that, what will be, will be. I spent the night on the sofa but did not sleep too well as I had things to resolve.

Angela was by then settled in a flat just down the road from me. I saw her most days. She had two flatmates. Although the flat only had one bedroom it was huge, probably the old dining room of this old Victorian building. The flatmates provided extra cash to pay the bills. I was pleased she had them as they often went out at night to a bar or just chilled at home together watching TV. They were good company for her, as I could not always be there for obvious reasons. I was in an awkward predicament but luckily the nights I worked the clubs seemed to satisfy her needs. On a Sunday morning I would jog over and sneak into her bed, usually after taking in an eyeful of her semi-naked flat mates, hanging out of their beds. We would have sex and I can't think of one instance that the other girls made a sound or joined in.

My passion for singing was now making me good money. I had several agents who got me regular gigs throughout the North of England, sometimes two clubs a night. It was bringing in much needed extra cash and giving me time needed with Angela.

 After a year in Manchester, Angela got her own house. She cooked for me at least once each week and as well as being my lover, she also became my seamstress, running up stage outfits.

I was investing in my image. I wanted to be different, stand out from the crowd. I did. Some cat-suits even see-through.

Now in her own space, I began to see a different side to her. She was a good cook, but very untidy and certainly no slave to housework. She was drinking a lot and putting on weight, mainly because of me and my absence.

She was pressurising me to leave my wife. I had to do something! I had two young children now and I was neglecting my day job. I was in trouble. How the wheels turn! The company car, new only just over two years ago was shot, the job was less than stimulating and to be truthful, so was Angela.

It was the middle of November. (I do stupid things this time of the year) Taking the bull by the horns, I rang head office and resigned. They asked me to take the car and customer files back to Howden, some hundred miles from home. I hadn't told them about the state of the car. I had no choice but to ask Angela to follow me up the M62 motorway, with a sick car running on three cylinders, and be there for me for the return journey. The day was awful. In tune with my mood, it rained all the way. It was cold and the car packed up about twenty miles from the factory and had to be towed the last few miles.

I didn't hang around in Howden. I was not in the mood for explaining my actions, or the condition of the car. The return journey was also bleak, the hood on the MG letting in the icy rain.

Cold, wet and very depressed, we arrived at her house late afternoon. Angela ran a bath and switched on the electric blanket. We lowered ourselves carefully into the steaming bath, both in our own private worlds, silently washed away the dreadful day and climbed wearily into bed. Silence hung heavy around us, the unspoken speaking volumes. Without tears or recriminations, we both knew it was the beginning of the end.

Gradually my double life got a little easier as our relationship entered a new phase. Angela was still around. She had got to know lots of musicians that I was working with and managed bookings for me as well as making some of my now much talked about stage gear. We both knew our affair was over, but we were still good friends and continued helping each other.

I got a new job. Sales again, and the best thing of all was that the office was less than five miles away from home. I had a great boss, Ted. We would finish the day, if we were both back at the office, around five pm and go down the local bar.

This was before the UK drink and drive laws were fully implemented in 1983, so we would get smashed at least twice a week and then again on a Friday. How we got home those nights, driving our company cars, I will never know. It got so bad that on occasions my wife would appear with my evening meal and slam it down on the bar!

Ted was good at his job. I was learning his skills and becoming his equal. He had a wife and daughter and also a long lasting love affair with a woman down in Bristol. He was more than happy with my sales figures and we were above our targets with lots of orders in the pipeline, so there were no concerns regarding the late night gigs etc.

 It was June, with the winter blues behind me. I was a happy guy generally, now especially, always nice and friendly with colleagues in the office, three middle-aged ladies and a pleasant young woman on reception, Sandra. I flirted with them all.

Ted was away for the day, I remember. We shared the same office. Being next to the workshop, we used to keep the door closed because of the noise.

I was on the phone to a client when the door opened and in walked Sandra off reception. Medium height with ash blonde hair, large glasses, (the latest fashion), a knee-length denim dress. She closed the door firmly, leaned sugestively back against it and began to pull open the metal poppers on her dress, which went right down the front. Grinning, she revealed her bra and on down to her panties. With a long, lingering, meaningful look, she stayed like that for a few seconds before fastening her dress back up and leaving the office. I was still on the phone, entranced.

I finished my call and laughed to myself – what the fuck just happened? I went out into the main office to the kitchen to make a cup of tea and sure enough, she followed.

"Why?"I asked.

"I had to make a move. God! Did you not realise I wanted to talk?"

"But we do - we talk all the time," I said.

"Yes, and you always just thank me for doing things for you. I want to do more."

I grabbed my tea, extricated myself gingerly from the kitchen and escaped to my office, working until the girls had all gone, not wanting to confront her again. I walked into the workshop, had a chat with some of the mechanics, still preparing some machines, then walked across to my car and, headed home to be greeted with a kiss from my wife and hugs from my young daughters. Karen was now around five years old and Samantha a year younger.

I played games with them for a while before eating, then put them to bed, the events earlier in the day pushed to the back of my mind, forgotten. As I said before, things were okay at home, although money was tight - when wasn't it?

We had bought a large Victorian house in Salford, on Claremont Road, a much sought-after address at the time. It was our second home and it was substantial . From the kerb-side, it looked like a normal two-storey home . Two large front bay windows, with beautiful leaded coloured glass panels were dwarfed by a substantial triangular fascia. Black beams and white painted panels decorated the facia that followed the steep line of the double pitch roof, the main architectural feature of the grand semi-detached house. This roof space created a huge attic with two bedrooms.

The ground floor had two large reception rooms, leading from the main hallway and stairs, into a dining room, via a small corridor, then another door into a single height section incorporating the kitchen and a WC. In total, nine rooms, five of which were bedrooms.

Every penny of our spare cash went on redecoration. The spare cash coming from my gigs, so this was important to us.

Life ticked over, lulling me into a false sense of security. It didn't last. One cold, autumnal morning, immediately on my arrival at work, I was summoned to the boardroom.

The old man, the managing director, who looked like Bernie Ecclestone, said,

"Sit down. I have something serious to discuss with you. Ted won't be working here anymore, he has gone."

It was a blow- what's happened, I thought? At the same time, I was relieved it wasn't about my other activities.

" What happened?"

"I can't tell you the details, but you must not contact him from now on. That's all for now."

Then two days later, I was called into another meeting.

"I want to give you the opportunity to take over from Ted,"

Well I was surprised and grateful, as promotion meant extra money which always came in handy. It was great news in one respect, but I still didn't know what had happened to Ted. His desk had been cleared, his car was in the work shop, and even Charlie, the works manager and long-time colleague was in the dark.

I needed to knuckle down to the new role and the responsibility. I was going to be the Sales Director. How would it effect my relationship with the band? I realised it was just me on my own now. We had an agency that covered the whole of Lancashire and Yorkshire, which Ted and I had shared. There was no way I could do it all.

The company relied on sales, as most companies do, to keep the whole thing viable and this was a family firm, now some fifty years old. I thought about all the employees, their jobs would be in jeopardy if I didn't perform. The pressure became tense. I needed help. Sandra on reception kept offering it. Very tempting, she did have a great tits!

I contacted Mike, who I used to work with in the last job. He of course lived in Yorkshire, Bradford - a good location. He was now a father, I contacted him, he expressed he needed a change, so we arranged an interview at the office and he was hired. Three months passed and we had great continuous success, yet despite everything I still didn't feel fulfilled.

I was scanning the papers and in The Stage magazine, I saw auditions were open for a musical 'The O Boy' stage show in London.

The following week I was driving through London by 8am enjoying the challenge the rush hour on heavily congested roads I didn't know. The morning was beautiful, warm and sunny, I felt good.

 I passed the House of Commons and drove over the Thames, the window open, a light breeze on my face. I had a good feeling inside, one of eager anticipation. I felt lucky. This was where I should be if I wanted to make a name for myself. I panicked I lost my way locating the venue but in the end managed to park and freshen up, using the local YMC

The 'O Boy Show' was a weekly television program and the first BBC TV show catering for teenagers. It was on TV in 1958 and lasted just over a year. It was produced by Jack Good, who had previously produced 'The Six-Five-Special.' He introduced the first British Rock & Roll stars to the masses.

I had watch these programs as a young kid, I wanted it so bad.

I had a time slot I got in line, so confident. I would say fifty or more people were in front of me, some warming up their voices, even exercising their bodies, and with a sinking heart I realised I was out of my depth. These people lived in London and must attend auditions every week. They knew exactly what to expect, they understood the process. I was here on a hunch. I would have to be extremely fortunate to be offered a part. However, luck was the name of this game. I was on such a high, I was even foolish enough to think I was going to get a leading part.

Armed with two sheets of music, the producer called me up to the piano. Around five feet six, slightly bald, a rounded, fresh face and impeccable white teeth. There he stood, smiling. He was wearing a colourful shirt. He had that aura around him, that special something, that swell of success.

"Your name?"

He took the sheet music out of my hand, looked at the title before handing it to the young guy on the piano.

Then, "What other productions have you been in?"

I explained that I had travelled from Manchester and I had been working the northern clubs.

He seemed interested. "Okay Norman, show me what you can do."

So with a cold voice, (what did I know about warming up?), I began. My voice was strong. I sang a ballad to show my control. Should I have sang 'Move It'? He listened intensely, right to the end, a pleasant surprise as previously he stopped other singers after just a few bars. I stood there expectantly, waiting for a positive reaction.

He smiled. "You have an interesting voice."

My pulse rate quickened.

"Thanks for coming all the way from Manchester. We will be in touch,"

He held out his hand and offered an apparently sincere handshake, yet I knew I would never hear back from him.

I enjoyed a few hours in the capital, knowing that I would need a miracle to find myself working there. I looked at the positives that hah come out of the day. It had all been good experience, if nothing else.

The same week, in the local Manchester Evening News, there was an advert in the classifieds.

"Wanted: Singer for a Shadows instrumental band."

Some guys, based in Stockport, about thirty miles away, had posted the request in the '*Bands and Musicians*' section. The guys were:

Alan Jackson, who lived in the Fallowfield area of Manchester and had been professional with a couple of groups in the early-to-mid 60s at the height of the Manchester beat scene. Rhythm guitarist *Brian Jackson,* (no relation to Alan), from Stockport. On drums, *Keith Newton* - who had for a time been with Dave Berry and the Cruisers in the 60s, also from Stockport, and on Lead guitar, *Graham Hamilton,* from Oldham.

This was the opportunity I had been looking for, to develop my singing career and cut down on the booze. It was achievable, not pie in the sky. They accepted me after a few hours of jamming in an upper room of a local pub. I had been singing Cliff songs for years. I had the same inflections in my voice and this was the perfect union.

Rehearsals began and very soon we had a manager, and performances in the pipeline.

I was doing one of my solo gigs, one of my last, as the diary with the band would soon be full. The night in question, I met a very interesting drummer, who said he had a recording studio in nearby Oldham. I explained I had several self-penned songs I would love to record. His name was John Needham. A session guy who had returned from London after working down there for a couple of years. I got his number.

That evening, after the local gig, I received letter from Dick Clarke, the band's Manager. I sat down in a daze with my wife and went through the upcoming gigs, with Vintage; Newcastle, Northumbria, Somerset and Yorkshire, serious stuff.

I was ecstatic. Finally, I was living the dream. My wife didn't share my joy; she knew changes were afoot.

She got that one right! The next week's rehearsals were intense.

John, the drummer called me a few days later, about recording a single. He had returned from London to play with an up and coming group in Oldham that had just lost their drummer. (writing this I made contact again after 35 years) He said that for the life of him he couldn't remember their name but it had led to him being co-owner of Pennine Studios then in its infancy, a small eight track set up. I went to see it.

I think it was in an old cold store, as I remember. The main room was big enough for a band to set up and there was a section which also contained the control desk and playback gear. Off the main area was an isolated room, accessed by a door similar to what you would see on a submarine or ship, much the normal size of a standard door but with rounded corners, made of steel and fitted with a large wheel, that was turned to open and close it. When inside the small room, it was sound proof. In the centre was a microphone sat on a very heavy metal stand. The room was connected by headphones for communication with the main studio room. You were isolated, quite an experience, especially if the light went out.

I had written my songs on bits of paper with the tunes locked away in my head. I had to get the music scored so my guys could play them. I worked with another keyboard guy quite a lot in another club. He was a great piano player. His name was Norman Crabtree. Until I approached him, to arrange the music for me, I didn't realise he worked at the BBC and by coincidence knew of John Needham.

Perfect, I thought. I sang the songs for him, around his piano at his home in Manchester. I think it was in Stretford and we soon had the basis for the written music. He was going to produce it for me as well. I had struck gold!

At last, a chance for me to do what I had dreamed of for some time, record my songs.

We set a date in December. It was 1977.

Norman G. arrived and began to organise the guys from Vintage.

Keith Newton: Drums, Alan Jackson: Bass guitar, Graham Hamilton, Lead guitar, Brian Jackson: Rhythm guitar, with Norman Crabtree on keyboards and directing.

We recorded *One fine day*, the A side and W*hat are you doing to me?* for the B-side.

The recording went like clockwork, first take on both songs were perfect.

"That's it," a voice in the headphones said, "Come out," As I did I got a round of applause. "I thought Cliff was going to appear out of the booth," shouted John.

I was delighted to hear the reaction but blown away when I heard the playback after it had been mixed.

It was as good as anything I had ever heard on the radio.

"Great job," Norman Crabtree said.

Everyone thought it sounded brilliant. It was a great experience for all the guys in the band and we had two new songs for our show.

I wish I could re-live that moment when we sat and listened to the playback. I remember walking out of the studio around two in the morning, my ears ringing and my heart thumping. It was a frosty, crisp night. The stars were twinkling away. I stood there on my own and gazed up at them. It was a moment of contemplation. I didn't feel the cold, although the warm breath from my mouth, visible in the cold air reminded me.

 I just felt fantastic.

I arrived home in the early hours.

My wife came downstairs to greet me.

"Well how did it go at the studio?"

In a lovely mood, she had had a bath and I could smell her perfume. She was wearing a thin, skimpy nightdress.

 I took the cassette tape from my pocket, (the songs from the session had been copied for me), and put it into the player.

"Sit down," I said, then pushed the play button. *One Fine Day* started.

I watched her face, as I held her close. She didn't normally comment about my singing, but I could see she was shocked.

"Is that you?"

I smiled and we went to bed and enjoyed each other, both on a high. It was the natural thing to do.

Shortly after that night she was pregnant again, with our third child.

The record *One Fine Day* was an important tool for the band, something to promote and it would bring in more work. Although some band members didn't see it that way. The radio interviews which followed, although frequent, were with small local radio stations but still created interest.

Soon after our session, 'Pennine' received a large royalty advance (not from my recording I may add. If only!), which helped them purchase a large church property and expand the studio. Among the names who recorded there were John Wood, (Squeeze), Ben Findon, (Dooley's & Nolans), Pete Watts, (Mott the Hoople), in later years, Joy Division, Lisa Stansfield and Jack Bruce, to name a few.

Pete Murray, a top DJ of the day, at the BBC, in London had played *One Fine Day* nationally and reviewed it.

The biggest hurdle was the fact that we had no distribution. It was down to me to get it into the stations, with some assistance from Dick Clarke, our manager.

The single was as good as anything else out there. It just needed airplay and a vehicle to get it into the shops. The music, or should I say the radio scene, was back then, dominated by the BBC except for a few commercial stations that were on the rise. How times have changed!

We managed to get airplay on the BBC's regional stations, promoting the single, weeks before we played in that area. It had the desired effect and boosted our audiences. But it was unlikely that they would continue to play the single after the interviews as they classed the recording as "None Needle Time." It wasn't distributed by a major label, so no matter how good the song was, if nobody heard it, no one was going to try to buy it.

I say try to buy, because unless I, myself, placed it in record shops and that would have to be on a 'Sale or Return' basis, it was impossible to get one unless you attended a gig. Thankfully at the gigs, they sold like hot cakes after each performance.

We just had to get a record deal.

John from Pennine rang me to meet him in Manchester. It resulted in me signing a publishing deal for the two songs with Willneed Music A new partnership resulting from the enormous success in recent months of Pennine Sound. We could be on our way to a music career.

Behind the scenes, John and Wilfred, my publishers at 'Willneed Music,' were doing their bit and Dick, hungry to make some money from the band, was also promoting the single around the various labels, the majority based in London.

One of the ways to make money then was to get the songs onto the 'Rediffusion systems,' born in 1929. The company introduced the first cable radio service from Hull in the north of England to customers frustrated by difficulties tuning into the BBC.

Rediffusion. The word, it seems, means 'Broadcasting again.' It was piped radio and television. This system went to many countries but was also installed in factories, commercial buildings like supermarkets and they used lots of unknown music, especially for background, piped music.

We got on the system and I would often get phone calls from friends saying they had heard *One Fine Day* while shopping at the supermarket.

This and other airplay resulted in my first royalty payment.

I returned to pennine to record, I saw a man and Sandra.

Wilneed music had seen potential in the instrumental score of the 'B' side. 'What are you doing to me?' It had been scheduled to be recorded by the Manchester Philharmonic for BBC, but the recording session did not allow the time for it to be included on the day. Fuck! Another missed opportunity that could have changed my life. Another, if only, moment!

Vintage and Myself Centre.

Left rear. Brian Jackson. Right rear. Keith Newton

Front left. Graham Hamilton. Front right. Alan Jackson

(Written while courting my wife)

One Fine Day

One fine day your gonna be the one
To give you everything I want
You and I on a star so high
Loving till the I die
The world we know is a funny place
And you're my choice of the human race
I am taking you to my private star
To lock you in my loving tour
Would you like to come with me?
Join my world of harmony?
Sing my song every day and very soon
We will be on our way

Chapter 4

Work or pleasure?

A week at The Webbington Country Club, Somerset.

I booked a week off work to go to The Country Club gig and used the opportunity to take my family on holiday. The kids, all three of them, were singing "We're all going on a summer holiday," during the five-hour drive, to the West Country.

The Webbington Country Club was situated near Weston-Super-Mare, so I booked an apartment in Weston for the week. The boys were staying at the Webbington, but I wanted to keep business and pleasure separate. However, the boys didn't seem to be doing that as they were chasing the female punters and the housemaids after the first night, as I discovered at rehearsals the following morning. The management of the hotel asked us to be a little more discreet. We also had a meeting with a representative from the Eurovision singer Dana's management, about how we would arrange the stage on Friday and Saturday, as she would be accompanied by a big band.

.

Dana, while still a schoolgirl, won the 1970 Eurovision Song Contest with 'All kinds of Everything'. It became a worldwide million-seller and launched her music career.

Outside her chart career, Dana had remained a popular personality since her 1970 Eurovision win. She had played the part of a tinker girl in The flight of the Doves, (1971), a children's adventure film starring Ron Moody and Jack. She also performed in summer seasons at resorts and seasonal pantomimes as well as performing at venues such as the Royal Albert Hall and The London Palladium. She was voted Top Female Vocalist at the National Club Acts Awards in 1979, just a year after The Webbington.

Incidentally 'One fine day' was put forward for Eurovision, by Willneed Music. ANOTHER if only moment.

The Webbington was a very well established Country Club venue. The program for summer included some club-land giants at that time The Black Abbots, Suzi Quatro, The Drifters, Jethro, Bernard Manning, to name but a few. This was great exposure for us, leading up to our well-publicised Buxton Pavilion gig the following month, relaunching ourselves with our celebrity guitarist who had been off the radar for a few years and had a massive cult following.

Anyway, I spent the days with my wife and children, enjoying the summer weather, and the evenings with the other children, the band. A little bit of fame from radio interviews was getting the better of two of the band members. They had had their hair permed, the fashion at the time, and started wearing dark glasses everywhere.

I thought to myself! What would it be like in a few weeks when our new celebrity band member was introduced?

It was getting up my nose, to be honest.

Wednesday night came around. The club was full. The floor show was starting with a striptease act that night.

It was a large auditorium seating five hundred plus. Three sections of seats were separated by gangways and two columns, each mounted with a spotlight platform. In the columns sat two guys watching the stripper's every move. Who wouldn't, she was fit. I saw a little more of her backstage, as she used the same dressing room as I did. She certainly wasn't shy. I was amused, but had been around strippers before, normally during the Sunday 'Men only' concerts I had been involved with, in the working men's clubs.

Around 10pm, the boys gathered at the side of the stage waiting for their cue to begin the first half of the show, a set of well-rehearsed guitar instrumentals from a decade of chart hits by The Shadows. We were a tribute act I suppose, before the term was popularised.

My cue came, time to knock out those cover songs associated with the instrumentals the boys had just played. I normally introduced the band members later in the show and promote the new single. However, before I had reached that moment I heard a voice shout,

"Sing *One fine day.*"

It was Ted my ex-boss. He made his way to the front of the stage and stood there for several minutes, a big grin on his face, before retreating back into the darkness of the auditorium.

I was smiling too through the rest of the set. I wanted to see Ted and catch up with him. We were called back for two encores, before finally getting back into the dressing room where I was expecting to see Ted. He wasn't there, so I changed quickly and headed into the main room. I looked around but still couldn't see him. The lounge bar? No, still no sign of him.

I sat down with our manager and had a well-earned drink. We talked about the night and briefly about the weekend including Dana, me all the while scanning the room, hoping to see Ted. Around midnight I left the club, to head back to Weston and my family.

Driving back, still on a high, I wondered why Ted had just gone without saying goodbye. I knew he had connections in Bristol and his girlfriend lived in the area. Maybe I could track him down *one fine day.*

It was Friday. We took second place to Dana, the star of the week and her orchestra. I was there to meet her. She arrived in a bronze Rolls Royce as I stood waiting in the sunshine on the Webbington terrace. I can see her now like it was yesterday.

She hopped out of the car. You could see she had confidence, a fresh-faced glow about her and a beautiful smile. She reminded me of my wife when we had first met fourteen years ago. She was a young, dark-haired, petite Irish girl. I was hooked. We were introduced and I had the pleasure of showing her the backstage area, while her management looked at the stage arrangement. We talked for quite a long time, about me mainly and the band. She seemed very interested. We were both relaxed and got on really well. Yet another, *if only moment.*

Eventually she was called away. Time to go. She leaned forward and kissed me on the cheek.

 "See you tonight," she said.

 I got back in my car and drove back to Weston, where my sister, about twelve at the time, had arrived with my parents. Willing babysitters, this gave my wife the chance to go to the show that night.

That afternoon my sister made me climb up a very steep headland above the beach. She insisted both my father and I go up there, to the top. Once there, we looked down onto the vast shallow beach below and all was revealed. She had painstakingly written my name in huge letters in the sand. Bless!

The show went really well and the night was excellent. Our performance and Dana's provided a great evening's entertainment for all. Backstage was busy with people trying to chat with everyone involved and I got the chance to introduce my wife to Dana, which pleased her.

We said our last goodbyes and headed back to the kids and family at the apartment. It was quite late. We chatted about the night's events, said good night to my parents and retired. I remember it well! We made love that night very quietly. With three children in bed close by, it seemed the perfect end to the day.

I wanted so much out of life and I had to find a way to do it with limited resources and with a limited education. This was certainly a good period in my life and I was enjoying it, with lots to look forward to.

 The following night, Saturday, was our final night at the Webbington, and it was another excellent night. A full house and happy punters. I was looking to connect with our star again. She was looking at me across the room, as she talked to lots of people, and eventually I got the opportunity of a photo shoot together by the house photographer. I held her tightly around the waist, pulling her as close to me as I could. Despite our physical proximity however, the closeness that we had experienced during our previous meeting wasn't there. Had I imagined it? Or maybe things had changed after meeting my wife the previous night.

Sunday morning, we called in at The Webbington, said our goodbyes to all staff and the boys, then headed back home leaving my parents and my sister to enjoy a few more days in the south.

Dick, our manager, had been promoting us and we had several radio interviews that week. It was looking as if there were busy times ahead.

 We managed to squeeze in a family holiday, good for all of us to have a break. My relationship with my wife was fine and we actually got round to discussing the future and making plans. I was very confident about everything. How could anything possibly go wrong? Things were looking up.

However, the first day back to work, I was feeling a little apprehensive. It did seem a little quiet in the workshop. I had arrived early before the office staff. I went to see if there was anything urgent on my desk. A weekly report from Mike but little else; maybe Anne, my secretary, had the info. I read Mike's report. He had had a good week it seemed. There were three interesting quotations for machines.

Suddenly the main door to the office opened and the girls tripped in. We chatted about my week and I mentioned I had seen Ted, but not managed to talk to him.

 Later that week, the band and I had an interview scheduled on Piccadilly Radio in Manchester, a very popular commercial station, but they only played a snippet of the song. They were more interested in the story behind how we had acquired our celebrity guitarist, '*Jet Harris*', from The Shadows.

"How did you find him?"

The question was directed at me, so I told the story, in brief, then they interviewed Jet and finally Brian got a chance to talk. He had been breathing over my shoulder, the breaths getting shorter as his frustration built up. It had been his idea to find our celeb. So naturally he wanted to be spokesman.

We were promoted as *Norman Jay & Vintage,* both parties keepingl their own identity. But the guys would have preferred the reverse, and what I didn't know was that they were considering bringing someone else into the line-up.

 I was asked to take a trip to Gloucestershire to interview Jet Harris. Oh Boy, more weekends away now. Sometimes Angela would accompany me. It wasn't a problem for the boys, as two of them often pulled women on the night and the old van carried a mattress. It served two purposes. The first, was to protect the gear, providing a soft base against bad roads and large potholes. Occasionally when we were, doing long distance, I would travel in the van. However, it was more likely I would drive my own car and take two of the guys with me. Often the van and the gear had gone to the venue in the day with the boys, who were not in a full-time job. They would then set up for the evening show, which took quite some time, as we had a lot of gear now.

When I did travel alone with the band, I would never get involved with any women, one night stands, not my style. I needed to get to know my women. It was a confidence thing. Although I do remember having a knee-trembler, in a back street after a night on *The Royal Iris*, a ship that used to do night cruises on the River Mersey in Liverpool. It would be packed with young girls, screaming at the live local Liverpool bands, playing on stage. It was the nearest thing I ever got to a den of iniquity. That was before I was married.

Talking about dens of iniquity reminds me of the trip in the old Bedford van to Norfolk. Crammed in the old bus, five guys, guitars amps, and sound equipment. Okay, in those days we just had the basic gear and took turns sitting on amplifiers. It took Christ knows how long to drive there, seemed like days.

These vans had sliding driver and passenger doors and this particular van was thirty years old. The door seals were non-existent and the wind and the rain blew in for most of the ten-hour drive to the Cavalier Club, which turned out to be a dive of a place.

Recently, while writing this book, I have been in contact with our lead guitar player, Graham. It had been thirty-six years since we last spoke. He said something in an e-mail to me. *We weren't a 'Rock and Roll' band, in the true sense, neither were we really a 60s band (Beatles, Stones, Kinks etc.) Our 'thing' had always been the immediate pre-Beatle period (1958-1963) which was neglected. Therefore, we were hard to pigeonhole.* Despite this, he reminded me, we had been doing on average four shows a week and at one point, in 1978 we performed 24 consecutive nights. No lean feat!

The Cavalier was one of those late nights, where everyone just wanted to dance! We did not quite fit the brief, and we had to drive all the way home afterwards.

In contrast, the working men's clubs loved us, for them we had it all. Nostalgia, guitar instrumentals, with footwork, great songs and we were very visual.

The Blue Star club in Newcastle followed on from The Cavalier. It was a great club. We had loads of local publicity and the place was packed. Some of the clubs in that part of the country held up to a thousand people and this club was no exception. We did regular trips to Newcastle and Sunderland. We had a following.

That night I had come up with a publicity stunt. The single was doing okay, but you could never have too much publicity. I sprayed one of my copies of *One fine day* bronze, and put it into a nice glass-fronted frame. It looked pretty impressive. During the performance our manager, Dick, stopped the show halfway through and presented it to us on stage, for substantial record sales.

The stunt worked; the audience went mad and the rest of the night's performance was a breeze, with everyone dancing, several encores and a long queue to acquire a copy of the record.

The day job was taking up more of my time. Offers of gigs were coming in, thick and fast too, Cornwall, Birmingham, Warwickshire, and the southern counties. Also, to add to the mania, I was indulging in lunchtime sessions with the young receptionist.

I was burning the candle at both ends, running on adrenalin. Home life was good, the girls growing up, plenty of support from our parents. My wife did attend some local gigs when we could get a babysitter, but with the relationship between my wife and my parents breaking down, it looked like we would be losing our main babysitters in the not so distant future. The gap slowly widened, a slow, hurtful, damaging deterioration. A painful break up. I could feel the tension and it hurt me!

Chapter 5

Celebrity status

The weekend soon came around. Again, it was the northeast, Friday night, Saturday night, Sunday lunch and Sunday night. Three different venues, four shows, all travelling in the super, *new gig van,* hotel booked. We now carried about two tons of gear, money being reinvested into equipment, plus our Celebrity Bass Guitar man, Jet, was with us now. That was a good story for the press and we milked it. There was also a radio interview to fit in. The Friday night show was in Sunderland at *The Mayfair Suite, promoted as the biggest night out in the northeast,* another dance hall. Capacity, 3000. The promotion that night was a free *Pernod. Girls in suspenders however, got two!* Such a classy place*!* My thoughts drifted back to The Cavalier. Fingers crossed!

It was a huge room, so much so that we struggled to get a decent sound as we set up. We did our best. Empty rooms like that always reverberate, but with two thousand bodies it would be an entirely different story. Below the big high stage, a huge dance area disappeared into a black abyss. The upper floor was a mezzanine that wrapped around three outer walls, allowing you to look down on the dance floor, with lounge bars and seating areas.

It was always the same routine. The first half, the boys with the Shadows instrumentals, then towards the end of the 45 minute or hour spot, I would appear and do some 'Cliff'. This gave the audience a taste of what was to come. The second half was a maximum of three instrumentals then the full show. Norman Jay & Vintage, ('*Cliff Richard & The Shadows*')

This was how it had been from the very first show and it worked. That night however, would be different.

The first half would now include Jet, with several featured instrumentals, which he had written with Tony Meehan, the Shadows ex-drummer who "left," about the same time as Jet, who was still shaky, despite weeks of rehearsals in a church in Chapel-le-Frith in the wilds of Derbyshire.

It wasn't everybody's choice to have Jet join the band. Jet had been The Shadows' bass guitarist in the early years and was widely acknowledged as the best bassist in the UK in the late fifties and early sixties. He left The Shadows in 1962. According to the press releases of the day, he was going to pursue a solo career, as a musician and actor on the back of the films with Cliff, like 'Wonderful Life', and 'The Young Ones', The truth was, he had been sacked because of his unreasonable behaviour. It was Keith and Brian who had the idea, and they tracked Jet down in Gloucester, some two hundred miles away. Apart from Graham, we all went to meet Jet at his home.

We were all excited at the thought of meeting an idol. Plus he was joining our band. We had all watched him as kids, on television, and in films, with Cliff, Hank Marvin, Bruce Welsh, Tony Meehan, (The Shadows).

So it was quite a shock when we arrived at his address. A caravan park. He was living there with his partner. She was a nurse and was lovely. She obviously loved him very much but he was by then a seasoned alcoholic, (maybe his way of handling fame).

He was very thin, unshaven, shaking, unrecognisable from the TV personality of years gone by. While we sat on the faded sofa, he pulled a cheap Japanese bass guitar from under the bed, but was unable to finger it. This initial meeting, long anticipated, was a real anti climax, depressing and rather sad.

Keith and Brian, despite the problems we faced, still wanted him in the band. I was unsure but nevertheless saw Jet as a vehicle to more success, and so agreed it was a good idea.

The night came when Jet was to arrive by train at Stockport train station, to start rehearsals. Graham, who had not seen Jet at this point, as he couldn't get the time off work the day we drove to Gloucester, was the youngest member and he won't mind me saying, the least experienced amongst us. He had like us, grown up with the same music and The Shadows were his idols.

Eventually, the train pulled in. We were all ready to give him a great welcome, plus Dick had informed the local press, so there were some photographers waiting too.

And there we waited. And waited. The train pulled out and there was no sign of Jet. He never came. Not losing hope, I hung around for another hour, but no Jet.

It turned out he had been arrested by railway police and was currently in Stockport Police Station. He had been under the influence and when he told them who he was, they didn't believe him! So he was detained for wasting police time.

I have a quote from Graham from his personal story:

'We all experience disappointment at times and I've had more than my fair share, but I have to say that meeting Jet for the first time was one of the biggest of all. He arrived at Brian's house semi-conscious, dishevelled, looking at least twice his actual age (38) and smelling of booze and stale sweat. By the way, I'm not breaking any confidences telling you this - much more has been in the public domain for years.

I was all for calling the whole thing off there and then, but the others were adamant that they would give him a chance to redeem himself, particularly the spiv of a Manager Dick Clarke. So it was a couple of days later that we met in a village hall in Chapel-le-Frith, where Dick lived, to rehearse. By then Jet had sobered up and was much more presentable, though his face was almost that of a zombie, and his craving for drink was all too apparent. I can still picture Brian hanging a bass guitar around Jet's neck and trying to teach him "Apache". Unbelievable!'

It was time for Jet to appear for his first show with Vintage. This Sunderland dance hall, however, was not the best venue for his launch. It started well enough, with girls dancing around their handbags to The Shadows music, and with no seated audience, presentation wasn't so important. Our bass player was playing along just in case; the set went well, as did the rest of the evening. It was a relief to us all. I guess most of the audience on that night weren't aware of who he was anyway.

However, due to the press, radio, and our promotion, people would soon be booking to see Jet Harris with his band. The *new* billing was Norman Jay Vintage and Jet Harris.

His name now long gone, mine is still up there.

We made the headlines again, but this time with a different slant:

Jet starts a long walk back from The Shadows. Daily Mail, Aug 14, 1978.

Jet out of the shadows. Manchester Evening News, Aug 20, 1978

It became clear, after a short time, that there was little chance of Jet playing a full set, as our bass player. Alan (bass) our founder, wanted to play keyboards to make the sound more authentic. Another member was added, another young bass player, Adrian. They decided to use Jet as a sort of "star attraction" (my initial thought), the idea being, to bring him on at the end of the show to play his hit million seller's *Diamonds* and *Scarlet O'Hara*.

Chapter 6

Another page in my life

We made the papers yet again, well Jet did! Continuing on our build up to the gig at the famous Buxton Pavilion Gardens, we were booked to play on the Octagon stage.

The Octagon hall is the largest and grandest venue at the Pavilion. This beautiful Victorian room can hold up to 1200 guests standing. The Concert hall, now known as the Octagon, was originally designed by the Buxton Architect, Robert Rippon Duke and was opened in 1875. Now, it's a Grade II listed building and one of the largest eight-sided rooms in Europe.

Manchester Evening news March 1979 'Thursday Turntable' by John Stacy, '***Jet back on the fame trail.***'

Buxton local paper. April 1979, '***Travelling light Jet Harris***'.

We travelled the length and breadth of the country with Jet, for over six months.

In Cornwall I remember getting into a fight on a summer's evening, the beer going everywhere, whilst protecting him from a fan who would not believe it was him. He did look old for his age and the blonde quiff had long gone. People, I guess, look bigger on the screen too. He gave me an album that same night and signed it.

"Good luck for what we wish ourselves, Jet Harris."

None of us knew about it. It had been made at Gloucester Prison on 3rd April 1977, called '*Inside. Jet Harris*' on the **ellejay** label.

The problems for Terrance, Jet's real name, had started around 1961. *Carol Costa,* Jet's first wife had an affair with Cliff Richard, (*it is well documented. Cliff admits to sleeping with her*). This set off the riff between him and Sir Cliff. He left the band with Tony Meehan in 1962 and their recording of '*Diamond's* knocked The Shadows off the top slot of the top 40, with '*Dance on'.* He had a bad car crash with his girlfriend *Billie Davis,* shortly before a television performance on ITV's '*Thank your Lucky Stars'*, to promote another hit with Tony, *Scarlett O'Hara.* He didn't show up, leaving Tony helpless. Jet and Billie were later found hiding out in a hotel in Brighton. That's when things started to go very wrong.

Billie Davis had actually been to a recent concert of ours in Bradford.

Davis was managed by impresario, Robert Stigwood. She won a talent show, backed by The Rebel Rousers, Cliff Bennetts band. She met Jet when she was only 17. Her most successful release was 'Tell Him', which got to number ten in the charts in Feb 1963.

Rockers descend on Buxton April 1979.

That night the format was as the last few weeks, with Jet doing two or three numbers in the first half, then we would all do something in the final set, including a Rock & Roll medley with Brian and myself, with Jet playing '*Diamonds* and *Scarlet'*, before I did '*Move It*' and '*Please don't please'*. to finish.

We had a full house, eight hundred to a thousand people, the majority from the Midlands. The Octagon room was a large glass house with a central dome. The sound was amazing. We had hired a large public address system for this gig and a sound engineer and it would be recorded. Everything went to plan and fans of The Shadows were pleased to see Jet working again. They enjoyed the whole programme, including the new single. We had great support from the mainly male audience. It was a great gig. The radio publicity and the promotion Dick had done, worked. Coach-loads of guys dressed in Teddy Boy gear rolled in from far and wide. The band was overwhelmed by the frenzy of the crowd and the massive response to the gig. Heads got bigger, but they couldn't see through the woods for the trees, that in fact it was our celeb, not them or me, who everyone was clambering to see.

The weeks went by very quickly. More radio exposure led to more offers, including a big dinner dance at a very special location. We had also been to London's Tin Pan Alley just off Denmark Street, Soho, London.

I remember being in a lift that day with Burt Kwouk, an actor in Film and TV, of Chinese descent. He was in '*The Pink Panther*' films, and more recently '*Tenko*'. He played lots of comedy parts and did oriental fighting scenes. I wanted to jump out at him and pretend to deliver a karate chop but restrained myself. '*Kyai*'. Still a daft kid at heart.

We were left to wait in a small office; the window was wide open. It looked over the rooftops of the back to back buildings of Soho. There was little traffic noise. Papers strewn about, generally untidy, the desk was littered with record sleeves and a stack of cassette tapes about to topple over into the clutter.

The door was open to the hallway, revealing similar rooms. It must have been the height of summer; as I remember it was very hot.

We were there to play the single, adding to the collection. Dick was running the business side of things that day. I stood at the back with the others. A portable record player sat on a table near to the window. The A&R man lifted the multi changer up, and slipped my single over the little chrome stud in the centre of the rubber - covered turntable and clicked the needle arm. The anticipation as the needle fell and dropped into the narrow groove made my heart race. Truly surreal. I had visions of sound waves floating through the window and engulfing the London streets. The intro began and it was a wondrous feeling.

He seemed to like it. Someone else paused in the doorway to listen, as the song played in its entirety. Obviously worth a listen. On tenterhooks we waited for the verdict. We left with the words,

"Leave it with us and we will be in touch,'ringing in our ears.

We are still waiting.

That weekend was a special dinner dance in the northeast. It was about two hour's drive from home, and the boys had gone up earlier in the day to set up.

I arrived around 6.30pm. Then Dick arrived with Jet and another band member. I had been working all day and it had been a horrible, wet journey in wintery conditions. I felt tired and extremely cold. The venue was busy with people everywhere. As soon as I walked backstage, I was told that there would be a change in our routine. Jet wanted to do the first half. I wasn't needed!

 We had always had an order in the set, one that worked. The last few months, however, we had tried reversing it, the majority of the second half with Jet playing his big hits, then we would all be on stage for the finale, I would do the majority of the first half, with the boys, as we had done at the Buxton venue.

I was a little narked, a northern word for *pissed off,* but I accepted it and decided to make the most of the evening, eventually finding a seat in a very crowded hotel restaurant and ordering some hot food.

I waited about forty-five minutes for it to arrive at the table. Weary, frustrated and by now, hungry, I was just tucking into a nice steak, savouring the first bite when Adrian, the young bass player, yelled across the room.

"Norm, you're on!"

"On? Not me. I am on in the second half," I replied.

 "Change of plan. Jet has changed his mind."

The fact was, he had started on the booze, earlier in the day. I didn't know that at the time. But it didn't matter. I had had enough of the disruption, caused by Jet and his drinking.

I slowly swallowed that succulent piece of steak, before standing up and beckoning Adrian across. Leaning over him, my face close to his, I spoke quietly but firmly.

"Tell Dick and the rest of you to stuff it."

Leaving them to sort out the mess they had created, I sat down calmly, finished my meal and then drove home. I never found out what cracked off after that, but they certainly got the message.

Maybe it was my pride that was hurt. Could it also have been that I was getting burnt out? Too much work, too much travelling, a wife suffering from anti-natal depression and the general pressure of family life? Plus it's winter! SAD.

Weeks went by with no contact from them and I had no intention of ringing. Stalemate.

I contacted all my booking agents and told them that I was working solo. I milked the single and got a deal for an album with a small label, SRT, started by George Bellamy, the ex-Tornados guitarist. The gigs rolled in on average three a week, the money was very good, enough to survive on, so I quit the day job. I contacted several local builders and started producing plans for submission to the local planning authority, working from home, using my qualifications in building construction and technical drawings. My family life improved.

My girls, Karen, Samantha and Sarah, were growing up. I was involved with them a lot more, being a chauffeur from here to there most weeknights, going to judo, dancing classes etc, being Dad.

 My eldest Karen was dating a nice young man. They came to gigs with me, he helped with lifting and setting up my sound equipment. He wanted to go into the police force, so we started regular gym sessions together.

Things were looking up once again. I was feeling fit, I felt good, I had started writing some new songs and planning the new album.

The weekend coming up looked quiet for gigs, although I had had a busy week with the day job. Weekends were when I showed off my music skills and got the adrenalin fix.

Friday night I went to the pub, and by 7pm on Saturday, with nowhere to go, I was feeling let down. I opened a bottle of white wine. Sitting there in the lounge, in a foul mood, staring at the mindless crap on the TV, time melted away. More wine and a couple of hours later, the phone rang.

"Norman, can you get down to Patricroft Working men's club, pronto?"

 I recognised the voice of an agent of mine.

"What's the cash on this one?"

"I will make it a ton for a one-hour spot."

"Ok Tom, you're on. I am on my way."

The money was good but it was never about the money.

I grabbed my music case, took my stage suit, flung my Afghan coat round my shoulders, and stepped out into the cold, frosty night, shouting into the back of the house,

"See you later, off to a gig."

I unlocked the garage, reversed out and BANG! I demolished a wing mirror on the near side.

"Shit! Bollocks!"

I pulled forward, straightened up and went for it again.

 BANG!

"Fuck!"

There went the other mirror. Fumbling around I managed to piece them together and sped off in the rain. When I reached the club, I had trouble parking squarely in the space.

In the dressing room the three resident musicians came in to see me. A good band, organ/keyboards, bass guitar and drums. They had played for me in the past. I was looking forward to the performance.

I had two set lists, both around an hour. I chose the cabaret hour, as there was another act to follow me. So I took the guys through the dots *(sheet music)*. Everything at that point seemed fine.

I could hear the compere on stage, introducing me as I stood in the wings.I moved swiftly on to the stage, swinging my arm, counting the band in, a 1, 2, 3, 4, four bars of intro and then,

"Yourera eeeyes ourrs eeys of a wooma en louvre!!!"

My mouth wouldn't work!!! A mixture of wine, adrenalin and frustration.

I smiled and held up my hands up, as much as to say, what's going on?

The audience was bemused. Lots of smiles appeared through the footlights, as I continued. The boys in the band fell about laughing and the compere doubled up at the side of the stage. They obviously thought it was part of a new act.

Finally, I reached the end of that short arrangement of '*The eyes of a woman in love'.*

Lots of laughter followed. Good humoured laughter, I might add and then I tried to explain the events of the last few hours that had got me to that point. They hung on my every word. The atmosphere in the room was electric. I threw in a few gags for good measure, eventually regaining control of my mouth and managed to successfully turn the whole potential disaster around. We had a fabulous show.

Around this period, I was working as a compere in a music pub in Manchester near Smithfield fruit market. I think it was called the 'Smithfield'. A strange place and I must admit that pubs were not my scene. This was however, at least five nights a week, with an array of acts which you wouldn't expect to see. Screaming Lord Sutch and his band, for one. Acts would sometimes do two or three nights. Rock and Roll acts from the old days like Heinz, appeared one week.

I think back to those lonely days in my bedroom, listening to the radio. One of the singers from that time was Ronnie Hilton. He was a big star in the late fifties; a crooner, specifically. I remember one of his biggest hits. The chorus went like this:

There was a mouse! Where? There on the stair!

Where on the stair? Right there!

A little mouse with clogs on!

Well I declare!

Going clip clippity clop on the stair.

'*The Windmill*'. A great memory for me, but after three nights, I had gone off it. Ha. Ronnie was a great guy. Told some funny stories about his life after a few whiskeys at the bar.

Paper Lace was another band, and I even hosted for The Marmalade, a true chart-topping band from those days. Remember a song by them, called *Cousin Norman*?

Reference to The Marmalade name comes later.

Lyrics to,

Another page in my Life.

With the things I know I'll make it
With the things I know I'll try
It's been years but it didn't break me
Oh how the years go by
With the things I know I'm happy
Like the memory of the song
That I first sang
Don't it seem like several decades
Blown away by drifts of sand.

But things changed today
Now you're back from being away
I've turned another page in my life...
Things changed today
Now you're back you're going to stay
I've turned another page in my life.

Now you're back no one can hurt you
You said the magic words today
Now the world will be much better
We'll find a heaven waiting there.

I want our love to last forever
And stay a fresh as April rain
We've lost so many years already and both of us are to blame.

Chapter 7

Stability of a kind for a while

With the band and two distracting relationships behind me, I was looking at alternative directions to continue performing and creating music. I had to find another avenue to feed my passion. I often think how successful I would have been had I concentrated on some of the business opportunities I had been fortunate to talk my way into. I could certainly persuade people to have confidence in me but I either lacked confidence in myself or my interests were elsewhere at the time.

I was on my fifth career move, working for a radiator manufacturer based in North Wales. Again, in my first couple of months, I hit all my targets and established new contracts but then my motivation dwindled once again. I did the bare minimum to keep the wheels turning; to keep the company car and petrol allowance was always a bonus.

I had also set up a garage business with the brother of our bass guitarist from Vintage just before the split. Robert was his name. He would come along to the gigs and help carry all the heavy gear we'd accumulated. It was no joke humping tons of equipment in and out of the various venues, some which could be up several flights of stairs. Yes, he was our roadie I suppose, young and fit.

I had a little bit of a passion for cars and had just acquired a 1930s Austin 12, which he was helping me restore. Robert had recently qualified in bodywork and spraying and was looking for a job, so I put up a small amount of cash and we set up a car body shop in an old Victorian mill in Stockport.

"*The Ramp,*" we named it. The mill owner had utilised the old disused pump house which was about a thousand square feet to add to his business premises. Originally there had been no vehicle access. There was a set of double doors but I think it must have had a wooden dock or platform attached to it, so vehicles could reverse to unload. The area outside the double doors was restricted, even though it opened up to a large courtyard area, making the new entrance very steep, hence "*The Ramp*".

This venture, because of my relentless visits to car lots, produced vast numbers of cars for resprays and panel repairs. I was working weekends at the garage to help out and even recruited my father, who found the extra cash useful. With all these types of business you will never make a fortune and it would not sustain two full-time salaries. I took my cut for doing the books and because my day job was flexible, I called in most days to do some admin or collect parts.

The garage facilities also allowed me to finish my Austin 12 project, a 3 litre Capri. Then I bought a Jaguar.

The Jag needed a ton of work, including welding the suspension hangers, a full strip, and complete paint job. Looking back now, it's funny.

The mill was home to many diverse companies, which included several engineering companies, a furniture maker and two guys who restored car wheels, a technique called "Stove enamelling" which was a service we used.

One guy with a company in the mill had a series 240 Jaguar he wanted to sell. He pestered me for weeks and actually left it outside '*The Ramp*' one day to tempt me. I kept looking at it, but it needed so much work, so I didn't buy it. However, several years previously, I had the chance of driving my boss's 240 series Jag. It was fantastic to drive, luxury, a real head turner, so the thought of actually owning one was taking root in my head, especially since the Austin had sold and gone to Holland.

By a strange coincidence, over bacon butties and a cup of tea in the garage office, one day, Robert said,

"There is a guy here in the Express, (the local paper), selling two Jags', they're cheap!"

I sipped my tea without a word, trying resist my natural urge to jump in without thinking. But he persisted.

"One's a 240, the other a 320. How about it then? Do you fancy looking at them? Just think! A Jag each, parked outside the garage all shiny, a very good advert for the business."

That was it. I pictured the scene, convinced. It was a good idea.

"Okay, give him a call."

And the rest is history, as they say, done deal.

Both cars started and drove okay, but came without the current annual test certificates or special insurance, so we did what we did on a daily basis - took a chance.

We collected the cars one at a time together, and drove them back to *The Ramp*.

A couple of days went by. I arrived at the garage around lunchtime. Bob had put my Jag outside, to allow him to work on a customer's car. As I walked up the ramp I looked back at my car. Coincidently

Bob had parked it in the exact spot that the guy round the corner had parked his Jag, the one, I had refused to buy a mere couple of months ago. Something clicked in my head!

"Bob, come here a minute."

He picked himself up from under a car.

 "What's up, Norm?"

Pointing I said,

 "Do you recognise that car?"

He frowned.

"It's yours,"

 "No! look again. Do you recognise IT?"

 He thought for a moment, then we both burst into laughter.

 "Fuck, it's the same one from round the corner."

We spent a lot of time and money on our projects. The garage was suffering, so I sold my half of the garage to a guy I was sure would work well with Bob and inject some cash from his car sales business. It was the right thing to do. I had to get back on track, concentrate a little more on the day job before the bosses started asking questions about my activities. Specifically about how much fuel the company car was using.

So I knuckled down for a month or two to bring some sales in.

ClubLand had been good to me. I could always rely on making some sort of a living, from my gigs. The single was selling well and I had an album, 'Enerjay'. The album was complete.

We had two days in a small studio up in the northeast to complete the album, a very short time indeed. In hindsight, an impossible task to produce anything of quality. However, the opportunity was there and it was an experience, being back in the studio again.

The album was configured to satisfy the club land audiences that I was performing to, so it reflected that style of music.

I did, though, add some of my own songs, a new version of *'What are you doing to me?'* plus two more new songs, *'I saw a man'* and *'Sandra'* written about that little sexy receptionist.

Lyrics to **Sandra.**

S is for the summer when we discovered us,

A is for the afternoon, we first made love,

N is for the nights that we were apart,

D is for the days we were apart.

R is very simple, simply for the rain,

A for all my love, turning into pain.

There were some Cliff tracks too, *'She's a Gypsy'*, *'We Don't Talk Anymore'* and *'Please don't tease'*

I got in contact at last with Graham, the Vintage guitarist, and my keyboard player was a guy I had worked with on many occasions in different clubs and who originally was a drummer. That was the talented Steve Warburton. We introduced Steve to some new technology that session, a synthesizer. Considering he had not seen one before, never mind play one, he did okay.

On bass and drums, we had session musicians, Bernie Dolman, and Steve Bowers. Surprisingly though, we managed to lay down some decent tracks and with a little mastering, with very early technology, we put an album together.

 If you saw the film about Joe Meek, 'Telstar' you will understand. If you haven't seen it, I recommend you do if you like your sixties music.

SRT were a private label, and some months after I had finished my project they got into financial trouble, I lost their support, and it was down to me again to market the album.

I worked all the big popular northern, nightclubs and I was a regular at Bernard Manning's world famous *Embassy Club* in Harpurhey, Manchester. It opened its doors way back in 1959 and groups of people would travel from all over the country to its variety shows.

Bernard prided himself on the club's motto "*Clean club, dirty jokes*"

I loved Bernard. A nice guy, very thoughtful, unlike the man he portrayed on stage. In his own club he took the reins and when out there under the spotlight nobody dared move for fear of abuse being thrown at them. All very funny, though. The place was packed five nights each week, with three performers plus the boss. I was always on around 9.30pm, the middle spot. I would normally have been to an 8 o'clock gig and sometimes went from The *Embassy* to a late show, sometimes picking up around £150 each night. Not a bad little earner in those days.

The routine at the Embassy would always be the same.

The resident band, piano, double bass, and drums, would bring Bernard on for a couple of songs. He had a great voice. That's how he started in show business, as a singer.

He would then start with his Hellos, then his own version of the latest news leading to endless blue jokes.

 For instance,

"There was an old couple in the wilderness. The old guy was riding on a donkey, the old woman was walking behind, almost dead on her feet. A passer-by said, "Why is your wife walking behind you?"

"That's easy,' the old man replied. "She hasn't got a fucking donkey."

At some point every night, someone behind the bar would drop a metal tray on the floor and Bernard would say something about the thieving bastards who work behind the bar. The truth was they were all family. His mother was on the till!

While this was going on, the first act would be on stage ready for Bernard's intro.

The act was always a guitar vocalist. His instructions were to stand with his back to the audience, plugged in, ready to go. He could stand there for anything up to ten minutes, waiting for the line,

"Now Ladies and Gentleman."

I knew what was coming. I had heard it so many times before but still laughed with the audience.

"Well we have certainly seen some crap on stage at The Embassy and tonight is no exception!"

This was followed by more one-liners before the act was allowed to turn round and begin his routine. All good fun, part of the routine and certainly a winning formula.

Back in the cupboard, aka dressing room, Bernard would sit in an old threadbare armchair. He would tie a tea towel around his neck, after wiping his brow and face to absorb the sweat. On the wall, there was a makeshift storage cupboard, he was always mooching around in. Inside, pills, a comb, pens, bits and pieces acts had left behind, and on top, a small television.

 I remember it was a *Trinitron* 12-inch colour portable unit, with an indoor aerial. Always switched on, the picture usually very fuzzy. One particular night after rummaging in his little cupboard, he took out a key. Then told me about his recent trip to America.

He told me the hotel suite had been fantastic. He had had a great experience "but the fuckin Americans don't know what humour is."

I said something like,

 "They do now Bernard!"   I had seen the recent BBC documentary, where he had gone down a storm. They had never heard stories like Bernard's.

He held up a brass key.

 "This is the key to my suite at the MGM Grand Hotel in Las Vegas. I kept it as a souvenir."

 He placed it in the palm of my hand. "It's yours."

He liked me and would introduce me as someone that could sing. *"Ladies & Gentleman, now please put your hands together for a nice young man, Norman Jay. A singer's singer."*

Thanks, Bernard. God bless you.

He died in 2007.

I set a studio up in my attic room, just basic, possible with monies from the garage and a few good gigs. I acquired a Reel to Reel *Decorder,* (trade name), four-track recording machine from a studio who were upgrading, along with some microphones. I had a basic electric piano and a twelve-string acoustic guitar.

I have to tell you that after forty years, I am still playing the same three chords, as I did then and they're still the wrong ones!

The twelve-string, if tuned correctly, produced a big sound which covered a lot of mistakes.

I was happy in my attic, (good song title), losing myself in music for hours. It got so bad, my wife suggested we fit a bell or intercom system, so she could contact me!

I was out one night in Salford, a pub, the Poets Corner. A guy, possibly ten years older than me, was banging away on an old upright piano. Yes, despite the Jukebox being around, there was still the odd piano in the local boozers.

He was playing a song he had written which I thought had potential, so I invited him round to my place to use my studio to record it. A challenge for me.

Clive was a typical Salford lad, from a working class background. I wish I'd enquired how he came to play the piano. Maybe he was one of those guys that have a natural ability. He played mainly chords - his left hand just picking the bass note. They called that *vamping,* I think.

We settled him down at my *Yamaha* electric keyboard, which had several good piano sounds, explained how the auto drum worked and went for a take. The song was about our hometown Salford, around the fifties. Brian and Michael had just had a massive hit with *Matchstick Men.*

Salford then was a dirty old place, with hundreds of rows of back to back houses and a busy international dockyard.

After hearing the song a couple of times, I added the voice of my two eldest girls to the chorus. I can't remember if he ever heard that mix. He took a copy away with him that day I never heard from him again, from that day to this.

The song lingered in my brain for a few weeks, so much so that with my limited musical talent, I changed some sections and edited the lyrics until, The Salford song, my version, was finished.

Some of the lyrics from '**The Salford Song'**

I Remember Hankey and a place called Liverpool street,

A place down lower Kearsal where the kids all used to meet,

I remember playing football in a schoolyard of St James

Why did they have to move us, why did we have to leave?

Salford, Salford, Salford my hometown, it will never let you down.

Not a musician by any means, but I was producing recordings at home good enough to be rough demos.

I befriended a drummer, Gerry Harris, who worked at the Poco Poco Club. His son Lol, played keyboard, and although only sixteen, was able to write music and record soundtracks. He provided the musical score for the song and I began including it in my shows around 1981.

 I often tried to get in touch with Clive, eager to tell him all about the song, but in vain.

Many moons later, I realised why.

'Klive James' was in fact the correct spelling of his name. Technology to the rescue. I found this information via the wonders of the internet. He had, in fact, recorded the song, sponsored by a local brewery.

Around that period, I was working in Liverpool, accompanied by a mate, Tom. He was my roadie. All was going well until we hit the main road after a gig one night. Hundreds of police everywhere, shops on fire, petrol bombs going off.

It was the weekend of the Toxteth riots. I drove down back alleyways and across open ground in an attempt to find our way out of the troubles. There were road blocks and fires raging.

 Tom reminded me of this night several years later, calling me a hero. I had literally blanked most of it out of my mind. It had been a terrifying experience.

From news reports at the time:

Over the weekend, disturbance erupted into full-scale rioting, with pitched battles between police and youths, in which petrol bombs and paving stones were thrown. During the violence, milk floats were set on fire and directed at police lines. Rioters were also observed using scaffolding poles to charge police lines. The Merseyside Police had issued its officers with long protective shields but these proved inadequate in protecting officers from missile attacks and in particular the effects of petrol bombs. The overwhelming majority of officers were not trained, either in using the shields or in public order tactics. The sole offensive tactic available to officers, the baton charge, proved increasingly ineffective in driving back the attacking crowds of rioters.

At 02:15 hours, 6 July, Merseyside police officers fired between 25–30 CS gas grenades for the first time in the UK outside Northern Ireland. The gas succeeded in dispersing the crowds. In all, the rioting lasted nine days during which 468 police officers were injured, 500 people were arrested, and at least 70 buildings were damaged so severely by fire that they had to be demolished. Around 100 cars were destroyed, and there was extensive looting of shops. Later estimates suggested the numbers of injured police officers and destroyed buildings were at least double those of the official figures.

Such was the scale of the rioting in Toxteth that police reinforcements were drafted in from forces across England, including Greater Manchester Police, Lancashire, Cumbria Birmingham and even and Devon to try to control the unrest.

The Salford song was not the only piece I worked on with Lol. That was just the start. He had the musical talent I lacked. It was the perfect combination of creative skills. We went on to produce about an hour of piano tracks, with some string and guitar sounds added, for the songs that I sing in the clubs.

I had an idea, I was missing that band sound.

Generally, in the 60's the guys in working mens clubs were not great musicians. In fact, a lot of them used to tickle the ivories in the pubs, still living in the fifties, many not able to read music.

Times were moving on, however. Sing something non-standard and you would struggle with these guys.

I had an idea which would use my four track reel to reel machine, with my new piano tracks including extra harmony vocals. Plus use the younger talented musicians, now filtering into clubland to play with the tracks. Remember, this was the early eighties when not many people had seen a machine like that before. Back then, the club's resident musicians would accompany us, like I said many old school . Some still used a piano, although *The Hammond* organ or an equivalent was becoming popular. If we were lucky we would have a drummer who could play more than a drum roll. Most of the drummers back then sounded like they were in a brass band.

My new idea, would mean me carrying and setting up a fair amount of equipment but I hoped it would be worth it.

Tonight was the night to experiment. After explaining the concept, I fitted both musicians with headphones, so they could hear the music. We started and the sound was fantastic, I was feeling certain that I had a winning formula but the audience just did not get it. A strange silence, almost boos. They could not comprehend the concept.

They thought I was miming the words and the boys were pretending to play.

We quickly went back to the sheet music.

How things have changed. Not so long after that fateful day, Karaoke erupted onto the market and took off like a rocket. Adults, kids, groups, entertainers, weddings, proms, musicians and wannabes all wanted a part of it. The irony!

When the truth was, I invented it first.

Ironically, some years later I helped to present a karaoke slot, live on the BBC in Manchester, Karaoke on the Radio. Saturday morning.

Talking to another keyboard player, during a show, I told him about my tape machine, then spent the next week sat in a cold de-funked, morgue, working with him. The morgue had been converted into a makeshift recording studio, somewhere near Manchester. Richard Spanswick, the keyboard player, had written a pop opera. We were recording it, on my machine, doubling up to eight tracks.

I still have the cassette tape of the session, but sadly nothing came of it. Although I saw Richard a year or so later, while filming a video for me, I never had any contact with him after that. Until I found a link to his name, again while compiling this book.

His website says he was born in London before his family moved to the North of England. It explains about his keyboard playing and his video film studio and then goes on to say he was the musical director for Ken Russell's, 'Blood Brothers' and Stevens Sondheim's, 'Sweeny Todd'. He also toured with Barbara Dickenson and now lives in Oregon, where he writes music and books.

I tried to contact him, but sadly had no reply.

Chapter 8

Going East

I received a phone call from a contact I had been working with for the past year. He had tickets and flights to an Industrial Fair in Germany.

"Do you want to come? The hotel and everything is paid."

Why not? A free trip, I thought. I had been helping Peter set up several deals including an agency with a German company who had sent the invitations and tickets.

We made all the arrangements and soon I was to fly to Stuttgart. We arrived early morning. It was the biggest industrial show ground I had ever seen, with plant machinery of every kind. We walked with our cases for about a mile, through crowds of people, to find his new contacts at their huge display stand.

I had worked with Ted in this field of machinery, so I knew the game. The beer started flowing. We did the rounds together, eventually going our separate ways. I was in my element, looking at new stuff as well as catching up with manufacturers I already knew.

A few beers later and I started noticing all the attractive Fräuleins hosting the hospitality areas, with never-ending legs and inviting smiles. It was extremely hot, too hot to be suited and booted. As I start to feel the heat, something else grabbed my full attention.

A guy was giving a demonstration of a remarkable forklift truck, quite unique, so designed as to give the greatest possible visibility. Some genius had certainly thought outside the box!

I made sure to get all the relevant bumf and made my way back to our hosts stand, whereupon we were immediately led away to a beer festival in the show ground.

The German om pah pah band was blasting out traditional tunes in the warm, sunny, open air. Long rows of tables filled the terraced areas around the small arena. Teams of ample-bosomed Fraülines, carrying three fully loaded beer steins in each hand, efficiently kept hundreds of punters happy, offering Schnapps dispensed from a liquid measure hung around their necks, as chasers and Schnapps bottles hanging from their waist. German wurst was also available in massive quantities, so we drank and stuffed our faces, as the band played.

The next thing I remember is hearing my name. Slowly I came back to life, and realised in horror I had passed out in the toilets! Worse, as my eyes began to focus, my sense of smell kicked in, vomit!

Panic set in. How long had I been there? Had anyone seen me? How did he know how to find me? Questions flew around my head as I pulled myself to the sink in an attempt to wash away all trace of this oh so unfortunate event.

Poking my head tentatively round the door, I saw Pete.

"Oh thank God I've found you! Come on, we need to catch the coach to the hotel."

The two-hour journey to the hotel, in Aschaffenburg, despite the twisty mountain tracks, gave me the time I needed to get back on track. Thank the Lord for that coach!

Aschaffenburg is a city in northwest Bavaria, Germany. The area is not considered part of the district of Aschaffenburg but is the administrative seat. Aschaffenburg belonged to the Archbishop of Mainz for more than 800 years.

Showered, sobering up in my hotel room, Peter came to to say we were going to a club on the mountain after dinner that evening.

So, several hours later, dinner over, washed down with some superb local wine, we made our way down to the main entrance. Two white Mercedes limos drew up, we jumped in and held on tight as we went like bats out of hell up into the mountains. After around 30 minutes of rally cross, we drove through a quiet village and screeched to a stop outside a bar. Typically alpine, tall timbered buildings with large overhanging fascias surrounded us, a quaint, quiet place.

 There were eight of us, six English and two German guys from the factory. The bar was empty, a large, traditional, high-ceilinged room, with wooden beams, wooden floors and wooden panels around the walls. Oblong tables filled the space like a bier keller. There was a stage, with dark green and gold curtains, drawn. We were all a little bemused, except for our German hosts, who ordered the beers.

The Fräuleins, this time, young and slim, not like earlier, had short leather skirts with white tops, and set the beer down on the table with welcoming smiles. I immediately saw, with relief, they were just normal size measures. Thank God!

 Loud music suddenly broke the mood and the curtains opened along with our mouths. We all sat there frozen in motion, at the sight before us. At least eight naked bodies, also frozen like statues, in various sexual poses. The music gathered tempo and the sex show began. There was only one way to go and that was most definitely another round!

My life until then, had been fairly innocent as far as porn and the seedy side of life was concerned. Apart from my few sexual escapades, I had seen one solitary blue movie on an old super 8 projector, made around 1960. Something to do with Vikings.

That night was indeed educational, to say the least. Four couples copulating. three French hens, two turtle doves and a partridge in a fig leaf! What a night!

Some days later, after the German trip, back at home, still recovering, my mind wandered back to the unusual machine at the fair. I sent a fax to the company inquiring about it and a week later, had a reply from the East German Embassy, saying I would require a visa to enter the country and visit the factory. I hadn't realised. What now?

 I would need funding to make it work. I approached a friend, an accountant, who put me in contact with some people in the city. We set up a meeting and on the information presented in my business plan, they provided me with a letter confirming their support and copies of their public accounts, as part of my references.

 I drove confidently up to the Embassy of the '*German Democratic Republic*'. *Brent Cross House, 124 The Broadway NW9.* I felt reassured, knowing I had the support of a certain Mr. Silver, a Jewish businessman, and then suddenly a little nervous as electrically operated, ornate- wrought iron gates slowly opened.

 I announced myself, via the intercom and at once was ushered inside. I was treated like a king. Completely surreal, off the wall, out of the box, however you describe it, two ambassadors inviting little old me to lunch! Not your average Wednesday afternoon, that's for sure!

My hosts were Frau Schwager, a diplomat and her Director, Herr Riegg. He was a fine looking man, early sixties, around five feet seven, immaculately dressed, a little rotund and sporting a moustache. I watched him with interest as he put on his long pale coloured trench coat and trilby, which were hanging on a tall coat stand. Frau Schwager was also a very sophisticated, well-dressed lady in her late fifties. Tall and slender, she reminded me of the singer Marlene Dietrich. We went for lunch at a nearby restaurant.

The whole set up was straight out of an 007 film. Nothing felt real. There wasn't an ounce of anything familiar to cling on to, to keep my head straight. The adrenalin was pumping in my body, as it did when I was on stage. Maybe I was on stage? Perhaps that was what it was all about. The reason I had worked so hard putting the whole thing together. Yes, of course! I saw it then.

It was a it a kind of theatre. My whole life was one big show!

Later back at The Embassy, seemingly impressed. they checked my credentials and called Mr. Silver. All went well and a deal was struck. As I waited for the gates to open before setting off back to Manchester, I discreetly let out a whoop of victory.

Several days went by before I received a letter from Frau Schwager, approving my visa. Soon an appointment with the Director of the factory in East Berlin would be arranged. In preparation I taught myself a little German, just the very basics.

The following month I landed in West Berlin. Too overwhelmed to ask for help, I found my way to Checkpoint Charlie and walked across into the East. There was a large, imposing, in your face sign saying,

YOU ARE LEAVING THE AMERICAN SECTOR.

It sent a shiver down my back. The hundred yards or so to cross the border seemed like a lifetime.

You're being watched every step of the way, armed guards standing to attention at strategic positions. If you go through on foot you have to pass through a small gate house. The door closes behind you as you enter and locks automatically – you're totally enclosed.

I was feeling sick inside. It was a small sterile space - no windows. The walls were stainless steel, totally lacking any detail. The guard behind a glass window, eyed me up, checked my Visa and stamped my passport. Eventually, a buzzer sounded, breaking the silence and finally I stepped through into the East.

I walked along Friedrich Straße over bridges, past the Brandenburg gates, down the beautiful tree-lined 'Unter den Linden', following a basic map. Spectacular. The Berliner Dom on the banks of the river and other glorious sights.

It was a beautiful day in May, pre-summer, exiting SAD mode. East Germany had a very low crime rate, so it was a relatively safe place to visit. I stared up at the towering terraced buildings, which lined the streets in the old quarter, and noticed the bullet-riddled stonework scattered around windows creating menacing frames and a constant memory of the past. Strangely eerie.

I was booked in at the The Hilton, on Mohren Strasser, one of the capital's finest. On check-in, my passport was taken, to be returned in twenty-four hours.

The room had a huge bed. Walls panelled in teak with matching furniture. Luxurious by any standards. It was 1983 and cost £90 for a single night! I took a beer from the minibar, slid back the curtains and stood looking out across the rooftops.

I received a call to my room, confirming I would be picked up in two hours. I showered, put my best suit on, making sure my shoes were shiny, my mother's voice echoing in my head as I did so.

"Always have clean shoes if you want to make a good impression."

Down in reception, I was directed to a taxi waiting outside. Sliding into the back seat, we set off for the factory. Traffic was heavy, streets lined with cars. The most prevalent, the Trabant, an East

German car, little known in the West. It was made mainly from compressed cardboard - it's true! Then there were Skodas and other Russian makes and models. The taxi was a black Mercedes.

We pulled up outside a grey three-story building, which was part of the factory. I stepped inside and found myself in reception. The receptionist didn't speak, but pressed a buzzer and I heard footsteps approaching, echoing down a long corridor.

This place was circa 1900s. Nothing had changed since then. Dark wood floors, brown and green paint on the walls and huge glass lights hanging from high-vaulted ceilings. Everything was spotless, however. The floors shone and shafts of daylight danced around the hallway, shooting in through the tall, elongated windows.

The footsteps got louder. I turned to see a shapely blonde in stilettos walking towards me, smiling and holding her hand out to greet me.

"I'm Helena, I will translate for you. Welcome to Takraf."

I was taken to the next floor down a long corridor into a room with a large table.

"Please sit here for a moment."

I sat near an open window facing the door. The rays of the sun illuminated the space. I listened to the noise of the traffic in the background while I looked around the room. It had a ceiling with beautiful plasterwork, oak panelled walls and the door, which was at least seven feet high, was resplendent with wonderful carved panels. The desk I was sat at was polished to a high, deep gloss shine. So old, I was afraid to touch it.

Four bottles of water and four glasses were set in a precise pattern in the centre. The chairs were large and heavy, covered in red hide. Nothing had changed here since the 1930s.

Forgive me but the names of the directors, I was about to meet escape me. I remember Helena's name for reasons that will become clear.

As the meeting progressed I started to understand bits of the conversation. Helena was brilliant, explaining everything in detail. I was invited on a tour of the factory.

I had visited many factories in the UK, and there had been a lot of changes over the years. There in East Berlin I stared around in disbelief . It was so antiquated. The machine I was interested in also had a little bit of old school engineering, but that was good in one sense, as it was easy to work on. It was the concept that was unique; that's why I was there. But they told me it wasn't made in that factory and that I would have to go to Leipzig to see it!

I took photographs anyway as I walked around, with their full permission of course.

Back in the boardroom, over coffee, a newly-prepared document was presented to me, a contract for me to have exclusive rights in the United Kingdom for my *Takraf* machine. My 'Gabelaufzug lastkraftwagen,' fork lift truck. Result!

We shook hands and I was invited for drinks later that night. I was to be collected by one of the directors, the following day and driven to Leipzig.

Back at the hotel early evening, I went walkabout. Wandering through the back streets of East Berlin was fascinating. Nothing about the buildings left standing after the Second World War had changed. Sure, lots of buildings had been rebuilt in the same style so as to blend in, but the original ones still had the bullet holes.

I eventually had dinner in the restaurant attached to the hotel. The meat tasted particularly good, the best I'd eaten for a long time and excellent service - my table was attended by four people.

Back in my room the telephone rang. My taxi was waiting. I was taken to another building on the outskirts of the city. It became clear it was the factory club, basically one room with an outside courtyard area, enclosed by high walls. You could clearly see the stars on that warm, spring evening, nothing else. I was asked if I would like a beer - I was obviously expected. I was directed to a table with about five or six other guys, dressed in casual clothes with a sixties look about them. They all smoked. Manchester United were the only words I understood, as they talked, plumes of smoke projecting upwards through their teeth. To be fair, a little bit of English was spoken and I tried to offer some German in return. Then, through the smoke-filled room, Helena appeared.

Wearing a tight grey skirt with a light blue blouse, she too, had a cigarette in her hand and was accompanied by the director from our meeting that day. My heart was pounding. One reason was the relief that someone could translate for me and two because she looked amazing. She had looked very attractive at the factory but somehow, just then, she seemed more relaxed and natural.

They sat either side of me, as the other guys shuffled around the table. More beer arrived and we all raised a glass. I think I was the only one without a cigarette. I was offered a small cigar, which I accepted, not to be discourteous.

It was unlikely any other English guys had been there before me. Why would they want to? I was only there because of the mind-blowing forklift, certainly not everybody's ideal bit of kit. For me though, I hoped it would be my future.

On several occasions during the evening I was told that we were being watched. Sometimes in sign language.

I didn't understand about protocol and at one point took off my necktie and rolled it up, offering it as a present to the Director, as he seemed to like it.

Oh dear! Not the thing to do! With looks of disapproval flying round the table, and heads shaking, it was placed firmly back in my hand, as they indicated to me it was not allowed.

The seriousness of my actions and the importance of protocol hit me like a sledgehammer. I was in The Eastern Block of Europe. Those from the East could not visit the West. They had their customs, their ways. I was only allowed there because I would bring Sterling/American dollars into the country by exporting machinery to the United Kingdom.

'Stay on track, Norman.'

The night progressed. With more beer and the group became very friendly. Helena sat by me, extremely close, close enough to breathe in her perfume. Between conversations with the others, we chatted about her life. She was divorced, without children and lived in an apartment. I told her about my life in the UK, which seemed completely alien to her.

Reminding me that I had a long journey in the morning so it would be a good idea to leave soon, she then kindly organised a taxi for me, I said my goodbyes and she took me outside.

This time, instead of my black, shiny Mercedes, there was a noisy, little Trabant car waiting, pushing out clouds of fumes into the night air, with its little three-cylinder engine rattling away.

"Could I offer you a drink at the hotel?" I asked, hoping not to get my face slapped.

"No, I cannot go there, it is not possible," she said. "But you can come back to my apartment if you want." She walked across to the taxi and sent him away.

She touched my hand lightly and we walked two or three blocks to the high-rise building where she lived. We talked softly in the still of the evening, the only other sound the clicking of her heels on the pavement.

"This is my sector" she said "My apartment is up there," nodding her head. Her place was on the seventh floor.

The small lift inside the hallway was only big enough for two people. It slowly screeched its way down towards us, as we waited in the hallway. All the council-owned, high-rise flats in England I had been to had smelled of cabbage or piss. This place had a different smell to it, a mixture of stale floor polish, rosewater or old women.

We slid open the steel, concertina folding door, clicked it back into position and with a few electric sparks from the drive motor, began the slow ascent to her apartment. It shuddered and the small light flickered. We stood there silently, our bodies touching. I could feel her breath on my face as we looked into each other's eyes, both wondering, trying to anticipate the next move.

The key turned and the door opened to her apartment. Just for a brief moment, my attention was side-tracked by the sparseness. The little things we took for granted in the west were missing. It was basic in the extreme. Enforced minimalism, you might say. Nothing out of place, everything orderly and clean. Just a kitchen lounge area, small bedroom and tiny bathroom.

"Coffee?"

I nodded. "Danke."

She smiled nervously and almost laughed. I watched her slim body contort as she reached up to open a cupboard, exposing the toned thighs of her fine shapely legs. She put an aluminium coffee pot on the cooker.

Everything suddenly seemed to happen in slow motion. The gas hissed, a match was struck, the gas lit and with a gently blow the match died and began smoking.

We were both on fire. I slowly walked across to her and put my arm around her waist, pulling her close. With a slight cough, she gently pushed me back.

"And I thought you wanted coffee!"

Abruptly she turned away, extinguished the gas, moved back across the kitchen and placed her luscious lips on mine. Tainted with smoke, I wasn't used to the taste. It actually excited me. I responded passionately, too much so, and once again she backed away.

"I am sorry. I shouldn't have done that, Helena."

What was I doing, for God's sake? Was I mad? This was East Germany, where there could be unfortunate consequences especially for her.

She shrugged. "It's late and we have a long day tomorrow."

"We? Does that mean you will be coming to Leipzig?"

"Yes, of course. Are you suddenly fluent in German now?"

We both smiled. The second awkward moment had passed.

"We are staying the night there, so wait, Mr Jay, be patient," She adjusted her blouse, smiling sweetly into my eyes.

"Can you call a taxi for me then?" I asked, my arm somehow finding its way back around her tiny waist.

"I don't have a telephone." She laughed up at me. "Don't look so surprised. We just have to go down to the street - there is a phone there. Come on."

I watched her through the back window of my taxi as it puffed its way down the street. I left her, standing, illuminated, with the soft glow from the sodium street lamp. What a day I'd had.

The following morning we met at 8.30 outside the Hilton. It was a dull morning. We had a three or four-hour journey ahead of us. I spotted Helena in the car with the director. He was driving a Wartburg. (This mark and model of car did sell for a while in the UK in the 80s along with the Lada, which was almost the same except the Wartburg had a 2 stroke engine. A step up from a Trabant but a million miles away from a Ford Escort.)

Helena got out of the car for a moment with a smile, and quickly explained the journey, while moving to the rear seat, allowing me ride up front.

The roads in East Germany were not the best, believe me. Many were cobbled. They glistened in the rain as we did a steady sixty, in a very noisy car. It was hard to have a conversation because of the noise. After an hour we stopped at a roadside cafe, which was a real eye-opener for me. I thought I was back in the fifties. However, the breakfast was superb.

For the rest of the journey it rained most the way, which prevented me enjoying the scenery, and added a real moody atmosphere to the industrial towns as we passed through. I was excited about seeing my machine in production. After all, I now had the exclusive agency for it in the UK and I just knew I could sell it.

Involuntarily, my mind kept flitting back to Helena. I was so close to her, I could feel her breathing behind me. I wanted to turn around and look at her, but I knew I shouldn't.

They both smoked most of the way, so on top of a noisy engine, there was my slightly open window, allowing in some clean air. Even if we had needed to talk business it would have been impossible. We drove on in silence.

Eventually, we reached Leipzig, a maze of cobbled streets and magnificent buildings everywhere. We passed the railway station with its huge curved roof line and I had an idea. I would travel back to Berlin by train. It had to be healthier and quicker. The Hilton was only a couple of minutes walk from the main station in Berlin on Fredrick Strasse. Yes. I decided.

The tour of the factory went well. I was happy with everything. It was a little more modern than the Berlin factory and we concluded that we would ship the units without engines, meaning I could buy and fit more popular Japanese Isuzu engines, more suitable for the UK market.

That night we were staying in a hostel next to The Opera House. As I changed for dinner, I listened to an orchestra playing through my open window, overlooking the main square. It was a moment of calm, in what had been a tiring day. I was looking forward to seeing the town. So after a very business-like dinner with them, I asked if it was okay to step out and take a few photographs. I was trying to be very casual, not to draw attention towards my infatuation for his secretary.

They agreed and I popped out into the night air. East Germany, with its low crime rate, was very safe. I walked the city alone without fear. There were guards in sentry boxes toting guns on most streets, providing an extra sense of security. One of them shouted at me for jaywalking. I turned around as I heard a raised voice and saw a soldier walking towards me, his rifle raised.

 "English," I shouted! "Entschuldigung."

I got a bloody good telling off, I could tell by his tone.

"Es tut mir leid!"

Apologising as best I could, thankfully he sent me on my way.

 "Danke. Danke schön," I spluttered, as I headed back towards the Opera House, a building that dominated the large square, with its magnificent illuminated fountains.

After my short escapade in Leipzig, I returned to my room, gasping for some liquid refreshment. No mini bar. Damn! Okay, water then. Could I drink the tap water?

The room was pretty basic, no TV, but at least the shower worked, and the single bed, although a little lumpy, was clean. I imagined lying there with Helena. I showered again in anticipation.

She didn't show,. Disappointed but not surprised, I didn't know her room number, which left the ball firmly in her court. Restless, I decided to throw some clothes on again and go out to find a bar.

As I was leaving my room , the staircase doorway opened. She was wearing a classic LBD, a short black dress, looking like a movie star. Bright red lipstick contrasted with her short blonde hair, her eyes sparkling, her nipples clearly visible.

My mouth dropped open as I whispered,

"Schön."

She took my hand and led me towards her room. As I followed her up the stairs, I had a full view of her curvy rear, which moved with a flick from one side to the other.

"Schön, sehr hübsch,"

Around forty-two, Helena was older than me by ten years. She pushed open the door to her room. Candles were everywhere, glowing invitingly.

"Do you treat all your visitors like this?" I smiled.

In the morning, I took one last look at her sleeping peacefully as I left her room. We had agreed on the escape plan. We had to be careful. My heart was heavy; Would I ever have an opportunity to love her again like that.

We met for a formal breakfast, the three of us. Over coffee, I explained that I would travel back to Berlin by train, as I would like to spend a few more hours in Leipzig. Helena translated, then checked the train times and confirmed the time. We shook hands and said our reluctant goodbyes.

The Berlin Wall, (Berliner Mauer), was a barrier that divided Berlin from 1961 to 1989. Constructed by the German Democratic Republic (GDR, East Germany), starting on 13 August 1961, the wall completely cut off (by land) West Berlin from surrounding East Germany and from East Berlin, until it was opened in November 1989. Its demolition officially began on 13 June 1990 and was completed in 1992.
The barrier included guard towers placed along large concrete walls, which circumscribed a wide area (later known as the "death strip") that contained anti-vehicle trenches, "fakir beds" and other defences.
The Eastern Bloc claimed that the wall was erected to protect its population from fascist elements conspiring to prevent the "will of the people" in building a socialist state in East Germany. In practice, the Wall served to prevent the massive emigration and

defection that had marked East Germany and the communist Eastern Bloc during the period.

Before the Wall's erection, 3.5 million East Germans circumvented Eastern Bloc emigration restrictions and defected from the GDR, many by crossing the border from East Berlin into West Berlin; from which they could then travel to West Germany and other Western European countries. Between 1961 and 1989, the wall prevented almost all such emigration. During this period, around 5,000 people attempted to escape over the wall, with an estimated death toll ranging from 136 to more than 200 in and around Berlin.

Back in the UK, the Penthouse suite awaited. I arrived back home in Manchester exhausted, a build-up of everything over the last few months.

The following Monday morning, I left for my new office.

The Penthouse Suite, King street, was my *'Taklift UK'* address. All thanks to Mr. Silver, my money man. Mr. Silver, a small man, late sixties, was around five feet five. He had many business ventures and was highly respected in the local synagogue. *'Taklift UK'* was registered as a limited company. I was a Director and now I had to go out into the world and sell the concept.

 It wouldn't be easy. I knew from previous experiences in the field. The UK mechanical handling market was slow to adapt to change. The driver sitting on the machine eight hours each day could be your worst enemy.

I set about listing all the companies who would be interested in my machine from the *Yellow Pages* and various phone books.

I also designed a brochure and was organising the print run as well as office paperwork and business cards.

I was assigned a secretary. She was very sweet, fast at typing and shorthand, and for the very first time, I had a computer at my disposal, but didn't know how to use it!

 It was early days for computers, a replacement for the typewriter, a word-processing machine, the internet was not yet available to the masses.

After a movie-style start to this business venture, a massive amount of self-inflicted stress was about to commence. There was no time to think about women, but they could be excellent for stress relief, in certain circumstances.

Instead, my relief came through my music. I still had some local gigs at the weekends; my passion for music continued.

Several months on, we had distributors and orders and everyone was happy with our progress. Another trip to the main office in Berlin was imminent. My visa was running out, so I had to apply for another six months. Frau Schwäger was dealing with it and she was meeting me in Berlin to be my translator. I had no time to think about women, but I was slightly distracted, wondering about Helena. Would I see her? Should I say anything?

Back in the East at The Hilton, I spent the evening walking the streets of East Berlin. The night was warm, and once again I felt safe. I was walking in the university area looking for a drink. I saw no bars. Then I saw light from a set of double doors in a dark official building.

I opened them, with caution, to reveal a descending stairwell. I looked down, over the wide wooden hand rail to several levels below. I started my journey, a little hesitantly, my footsteps echoing as I went deeper into the unknown. Two levels down, I heard a gaggle of voices. I continued to the third underground level. Light was visible through another set of double doors with heavy frosted glass panels, revealing a subterranean, dimly lit, a bar.

Not a club. A cold-looking room, not very inviting. Bottle-green glazed tiles covered most of the walls that reflected the lights in the room. Heavy, dark-tiled floors, possibly marble, directed my eye to a long bar, with a bowed frontage. Large brass rails ran its length, a foot rail slightly raised off the floor and a hand rail.

Voices echoed loudly around the room and the clink of glasses hid the sound of the door as it clicked back into the frame. I made my entrance. I didn't feel conspicuous until I opened my mouth.

"Ein bier bitte,"

A moment of silence followed, except the barman.

"American?"

"English."

I pulled a high value note from my back pocket. He signalled to keep it out of sight, reached for a glass and poured me a small glass of beer. Then he leaned over the bar and in his best English said,

"Drink it and go, my friend."

A group of the people in the room were watching. Uncomfortable, I drunk the beer a little quicker than normal, all the while calm and controlling my body language. I placed my empty glass on the bar with a few coins out of my pocket.

"Danke. Gute Nacht," I said, as I slowly made my exit.

After closing the bar door firmly behind me, I started my ascent. I listened for the sound of it opening again below me.

Thankfully it didn't and I knew once I was back at street level, I was safe out in the open.

I walked straight back to the Hilton. My passport was handed back to me as I collected my room key, which was a relief to know I could get back home. I decided to head for the lounge bar that I had discovered earlier that afternoon. It was a very classy-looking room, high-vaulted ceiling, lots of coloured mirrors with an attractive bar with high stools. It had been empty earlier, so I was hoping at this late hour I could maybe find someone to talk to and have a nightcap. A major hotel in Berlin should be buzzing.

How wrong could I be? A single woman was sitting at the far end of the bar and the barman was polishing glasses. I ordered a beer and sat at the bar. The barman wanted to talk, asking questions. His English was okay. I kept looking across at the woman. Very well dressed, overdressed, to be honest. Hair and makeup as good as it got, she was smoking a cigarette in a long holder with long white gloves. She kept swinging around on her bar stool, looking in my direction. I got it! She was a high class prostitute. She must have been officially invited to service the customers' needs.

Well, not me! I didn't find that sort of thing attractive. I thought about it for a second I must admit. I was intrigued but I was not paying for it.

In my room I found a message. Hoping it was from Helena, it was from Mrs. Schwager.

'See you at 9am'.

Unlike the others, she was waiting in reception for me. A diplomat collecting me from my hotel, that was something!

In the car, she asked about our progress and I found out she had a flat in East Berlin with her family, as well as her home in London. The car was a Mercedes by the way, not a Trabant.

We arrived at a different office complex, maybe a kind of conference building. One floor, sixties style build. We entered a room and I saw the directors I had been introduced to previously.

 No Helena. I felt under pressure, but kept calm and managed to impress them with our progress and sales brochure, and I had orders with me for two new machines. They showed me pictures of some massive mobile cranes, ranges up to a hundred tons in capacity plus open cast mining equipment, used for coal extraction.

"When will you place orders for some of these?" they asked, via Mrs. Schwager.

I hesitated. "What do you mean?"

Again, Mrs. Schwager explained, "You have the distribution rights for all these products."

I thought quickly and explained we were concentrating on one product at a time. That was news to me! To my relief, they were happy with the reply and did not pressure me further.

So I guess Takraf was probably one of the biggest engineering companies in Eastern Germany and I had sole distribution for all their products! I should have been over the moon. In actual fact, the enormity of my achievement and responsibility it carried, weighed heavily on my shoulders.

 I was back and forth several times over the next year. Progress was good on the fork lift side and mining equipment, not with the British coal industry situation. Sadly, I never saw Helena again.

Three years down the line, home life continued without trauma. The normal weekend gigs kept coming in, nothing exciting or unusual, but I enjoyed my singing. I was working hard building up the agency. It was a great opportunity for me. I was taking it seriously. We had a good order book and spare parts were bringing in an income as well.

 An order due to hit the docks in Hull hadn't arrived. My shipping agent had no information, so we tried to contact the directors of 'Takraf' without success. The Embassy said they could not help and communications broke down. I was left with no equipment to fill my orders. The shit hit the fan with my appointed agents and after a board meeting, we pulled the plug. Thankfully we were debt-free. Shortly after this the Berlin Wall fell!

It had been a great experience, all part of growing up! The worst thing that happened during my trips to the East was at Schonefeld airport. I was stuck there for over 24 hours, after deciding it was less expensive than returning via the West. It was a mistake. There were a lot of strange goings-on there – weird, expressionless people walking around.. I was approached and questioned many times, even interrogated. KGB? Most definitely!

Thank you, Helena, for the much-needed translations and the lovemaking. I still wonder if she got the books and The Beatles albums I sent her.

The destruction of the Berlin Wall, definitely was the reason for non compliance of our contract. The East was not the East anymore.

Chapter 9

Music in Belgium and a girl from Wales

A year went by. It had been a financial struggle. I bought a few cars from the auctions, did a little work on them and sold them, plus my old building contacts gave me some work preparing various planning applications. I also had a chance to contact my music agents on a daily basis and secured regular of gigs on the club circuit. We managed to have a family holiday and my eldest daughter got married. It was time for a different day job.

I went for an interview, with a company who hired shipping containers and portable offices used on construction sites. I had seen this big Scots guy, the managing director and was also a director of a partner company which hired commercial plant. I knew about mechanical plant but nothing about site accommodation. It was a good position, 'Sales/depot Manager'.

At the conclusion of the interview, in his posh, Scotch accent, he said,

"Even though you have no experience in this industry, I am going to offer you the job, because, in fact it was you who interviewed me!"

The new job certainly kept me busy. It was a company that was in trouble and down to me to turn it around. I was back in sales.

I was ready for the challenge, happier when busy. The money was good and the BMW was definitely a bonus, so I was focused. Within six months, I was relocating the company to new premises and rebranding it. A directorship was offered; things could not have been better. Famous last words.

Then I went away for the weekend to Belgium.

My very close friend, Ian, a little reserved these days due to married life and a successful hotel business, agreed to my idea of a boys' weekend away. Calm and mature these days, he needed encouraging. How very different from when we were teenagers and he was the one who got me into trouble.

We both loved our music, which included Elvis, The Everly brothers, Rock and Roll in genera,l and over the years we had been to several Cliff and The Shadow's concerts. We still enjoyed Cliff with his own band. So I made an executive decision to have a boys' weekend away, to see the new Cliff extravaganza.

Writing this I notice there seems to be a recurring pattern in my life. Around mid-winter, I always do stupid things and in the spring, anything can happen! SAD has obviously affected me more than I imagined. I wonder if that is why I hate Christmas? I had always assumed I detested Christmas because I was born on December 28th and usually only received one present to celebrate both Christmas and my birthday.

We left for Belgium, from the centre of Manchester on a coach. It was November. The coach was filled with middle-aged women, all devoted to Cliff. As we were travelling without our partners, they assumed we were gay. We said nothing to change their views, in fact, we probably played up to it.

Our destination was the ancient town of Bruges, its historic centre a World Heritage site. It was winter and cold, a dry cold. We were nearly frozen to death, walking around the old town, looking for a place to eat and drink. The beer was good and plentiful, which we enjoyed. However, due to lack of communication skills, we ended up having a strange meal, before catching the connection to the stadium. With a drink and a welcome packet of crisps, we settled down in our seats. Excellent seats actually, slightly left, off centre stage. The sound was superb and the power of the bass, through the PA system, was actually making our chests ache. We sat next to two young women, who also discussed the power of the bass during the intermission. I guess it had more of an effect on them, having more than a fair set of boobs each. We exchanged a few smiles and comments.

There was a saxophonist in the band , superb. His solo in the song 'Joanna', made my hair stand on end.

I remember the night so clearly. We came out of the indoor arena after a great performance, to deep snow everywhere. To make the journey back to our hotel, we first had to take a short walk to the train station, attached to the arena. A shuttle would take us back to the coach park near the airport. Then a short 20-minute coach journey to the hotel.

The girls followed us, unsure of how to get back to the correct platform for the coach park. That was easy actually, as there were shapes of aeroplanes stencilled in white on the concrete footpath.

"We follow these," I explained, "to our platform".

They giggled and got in the same carriage for the short journey. We exchanged looks, but few words. At the coach park we went our separate ways.

Heading back to the hotel, the driver taking extra care driving in the snow, with the coach now full of hyped-up Cliff groupies, I saw an opportunity to have some fun. I approached the driver and asked if I could use the bus microphone, normally used to give out information about the journey.

I planted myself firmly against the fake leather dashboard and began singing some Cliff songs. Starting with *'Livin' Doll'* then *'Summer Holiday'* etc. The oldies. After the first few minutes, I couldn't hear myself for the noise of the girls joining in with me, singing at the top of their voices. The bus was rockin'. I had never seen so many women in such ecstasy packed into such a small space. Thank God the journey was short and I was gay…

We jumped out of the bus, the majority of the women worked up to a frenzy. They kissed and hugged us boys as we crossed the snow-covered car park to the warm hotel. As I looked back, to keep a visual memory of the night, there were more coaches arriving, with other Cliff fans. Around 150 people, mainly female, promptly gathered in the hotel bar and the alcohol started flowing. I scanned the room and spotted the girls from the arena. Now minus their winter coats and hats, I could see them more clearly. Smart, well-dressed, women with full figures. I went straight for the one with beautiful long, red, curly hair. She looked stunning, her makeup impeccable.

Ian however, didn't share my enthusiasm, but followed me over just the same.

"Can I get you and your friend a drink?"

"Yes, lovely thanks," came the reply, with a voice so warm and gentle, it raised my temperature by at least ten degrees.

"Tia Maria with coke."

"And your friend?"

"That's my sister."

"The same for me," she replied.

Her sister was larger, fairly tall, with strawberry blonde hair and a very beautiful face. Ian obliged, walking off to get the drinks. The three of us sat down and I felt an instant connection with my redhead. I was totally immersed in conversation with her. I was hooked. I watched her mouth as every word came out of her beautiful lips. Lips coated with a shiny, deep-red lipstick, her eyes wide and sparkling.

I was, however, being distracted every few minutes by another woman across the room. She kept winking provocatively at me and eventually, passed by, leaned in and sang, 'I'm a Livin' Doll', in my ear.

My new-found female friend and her sister had scarcely got up to go and powder their noses when another middle-aged woman walked right up to me, offered me sex and pressed her room number into my hand! This was certainly going to be an interesting night.

After the four of us had a few drinks, my redhead told her sister that she was feeling tired. Then she grabbed my hand, stood up and dragged me from the bar area. We literally ran through the long corridors of the hotel, up the stairs, to the door of her room on the second floor. We kissed, me going with the flow, enjoying the thrill of the moment, but not really expecting more.

The adrenaline was at its height; nothing else mattered, no one else existed.

We fell into the room, passionate kisses, fumbling around in the dark, clothes strewn everywhere, and sank onto the bed, hungry for each other.

Later, much later, we returned to find a few stragglers sitting at the now closed bar. Holding hands, identical silly grins on our faces, we walked up to my room like a couple of teenagers.

Her sister and Ian were both there, and we said our goodnights, reluctantly letting go of our hands, so tightly entwined.

The next morning, I saw 'Red,' (my nickname for her), in the breakfast room and got her telephone number. It was more than obvious to us both, that this encounter would not end in Belgium.

We left the hotel after breakfast for the journey home through France to the ferry port.

Ian had to come back to my house, as he had stayed over the night before we left for Bruges, and his car and some belongings were there. I could tell he felt a little awkward around my wife, but he stayed for a drink and rested for an hour before setting off home to the Lake District.

At this point in my marriage we had reached a milestone of almost 25 years, with 3 children, all in their teens. It hadn't been easy, in fact quite a rocky ride on occasions and this wasn't the first time I had been unfaithful. Red however, felt different, and despite the distance, it wouldn't stop me from seeing her again.

Lyrics of a song about that night:

Belgium

Who would have thought, we could meet this way?

A cold winter's night on a railway.

Looking for the track that would take me back,

To the place just by chance we were both staying.

You came, you came into my life

On a midnight train to heaven and just thought

I was making my way through Belgium

The aeroplanes on the platform floor brought us together.

One night of love on a floor above my room was unexpected

It felt so good, I fell in love I never meant to

Yes, the aeroplanes on the platform floor,

Brought us together.

Two weeks went by. My thoughts kept wandering back to Belgium. I took a double take at every redhead I saw walking along the road. Stupid! I knew it couldn't be her but I still did it. I found myself writing lyrics about her, the trip, my feelings. I tried to ignore the hankering, the longing.

She had described the outside of her house during Christmas time in great detail. She had a passion for that festive time. Her words went round and round my head like a broken record. I wanted to be there, to enjoy the time of the year that she truly loved.

Me, a typical Bah humbug! I hated Christmas as a rule, for reasons I have mentioned before, plus it was commercial and too expensive. Christmas aka Norman was just a time to cash in on the clubs. It was for children.

That day however, I was on a quest, driven by desire for a beautiful, warm, loving, attractive woman from Wales. Having made an excuse to go to South Wales to see a customer, I was heading for Swansea.

After a long drive in bad weather, I took the exit off the motorway which I hoped was the correct junction. Immediately I was on a steep hill going down towards Swansea city centre, large 1930s semi-detached houses to the right, open fields to the left.

Just off the M4, she had said. A festive tree in the front garden decorated with lights. A high wall, tall iron gates. I drove up and down, staring blindly into the darkness.

Luck must have been shining down on me that night. What are the chances of driving 300 miles and finding that needle in the haystack? It was crystal clear; it was meant to be. I sat quietly for a moment, looking over at tall gates with a tree, all lit up, in the front garden. It was drizzling. The wipers squeaked noisily. I looked beyond, to the street lights and the coloured Christmas lights on the tree, reflecting on the wet surfaces of the road and pavement.

With slight hesitation, I picked up my mobile phone and called the number she had given me. Would she answer? Was she even there?

A soft, silky voice burst through my musings.

"Hello?"

"Hello to you," I replied.

Pregnant pause, then,

 "Is that you, Norman?"

We spoke for several minutes before I said,

"How stunning your Christmas tree is looking, just as you described it"

 Again, there was a moment of silence. Then, I saw the curtains twitch, all the confirmation I needed that I had managed to pitch up just outside her front door!

My wipers were still squeaking. I turned them off, the engine still running.

"Is that you in the car outside?"

"I found you!"

 "What on earth are you doing here? Drive to the end of the road to the shop. I will meet you there."

My heart was pounding as I watched her walking up the road towards me. Sheltering under an umbrella, she looked fantastic, her makeup immaculate.

I pushed the door open and she was back in my arms.

She told me she had been thinking about me a lot and wondering if I would ring her.

'My sister was right. She said you would call and that she had seen a positive change in me'

A recent divorce had left her with two young children and a house with a mortgage. The weekend in Belgium had been a treat from her sister, to lift her spirits.

We arranged to meet for lunch the following day, as she had left the girls in bed in the house alone. A few more passionate kisses and I dropped her back home.

A different Norman drove to the hotel, full of joy, heart racing, a stupid grin from ear to ear, a Cliff CD belting out on the hi-fi, tracks from the Green Light album, reminding me of that formidable weekend.

It was the first time I had ever been to Swansea. I had been to Cardiff some years ago. I remember it being very grim, lots of demolition around the centre, old dock buildings etc. Her detached 30s style bay-windowed house was nice. It had an open aspect to the front, looking over the valley, but was almost back to back with DVLA.

We had lunch in the new Marina, Swansea Bay. Time slipped away, as we sat immersed in each other, hand in hand over the table, wondering as we talked, if the relationship could go anywhere.

I was entranced by her red hair that gently curled around her face, cascading down onto her shoulders, her softly spoken Welsh dialect, and her blue eyes, that looked deep into mine. We talked for a long time, honest talk about our lives our partners, present and past, clearing out the baggage. It seemed as though we were both ready for a new start.

It was almost surreal. How could it be?

"I want you to stay with me tonight," I said, kissing her cheek. "Can you arrange it?"

She explained that her mother worked at a petrol station on the Mumbles, further down the coast from the Marina.

 "Let's go and see her. It's only five minutes away."

I sat in the car while they talked, I could see them looking over towards me, her mother acknowledging me with a wave.

Red came to my hotel in the Gower area of Swansea in a taxi around 7.30 pm. We ate, shared a bottle of wine and my bed. We made love, until the morning. It was as though time and life were accelerating.

The following day, I was introduced to her mother in person, and her children, who were very sweet. We picked the girls up from school and went back to the house.

Commitments dictated I had to leave that afternoon.

'What the hell happened today? "I thought as I drove back up the M4.

Every minute of every day thereafter, I thought about nothing but her. I was obsessed. Days passed. Things became intolerable. I wasn't the same man anymore. If I didn't come clean I would burst.

After an agonising morning, I spilled everything out to my wife over lunch and sat silently, waiting for the tears, recriminations, shouting. I deserved that at the very least.

Without looking up, she finished her sandwich, gathered our plates and finally raised her face to mine.

'The real thing this time is it? Don't worry, it'll pass. Tea?'

It was painfully obvious she didn't believe a word of it and was taking it all with a pinch of salt!

Not that I could blame her. I didn't have a leg to stand on. A couple of years previously, I had gone away on holiday with a girl half my age! Had my wife not discovered a negative of one of the photos and challenged me, I would have been long gone, driving into the sunset in my Mercedes motorhome.

Of course in the long run, my wife did me a good turn. I came to my senses, her bitter words racing round my head.
"You should be ashamed. Twenty years younger than you!

She literally shocked me back into reality. What in God's name was I thinking? But I had been besotted, and infatuation is responsible for many personality changes. I had been in a bubble of laughter and unrealistic love, one that has lingered around bringing many joyful and hurtful memories. Now I had to deal with embarrassment, atonement and start to appreciate the wonderful wife I had. Bless her, she put up with a lot.

She loved me. I saw that then and am reminded of that fact every time we meet, even now, some twenty years on. It's all in the eyes. Sorry Jo.

And so it was happening again. And this time, she felt confident to accept my state of mind, until it had run its course and I went back to her. Have my cake and eat it too!

I arranged another weekend trip to Swansea, whilst talking to Red, during our regular, nightly chats, from my office that seemed to last for hours, after everyone else had left. It was a ritual. We had been doing it for months.

I had been in contact with some theatrical agents in the Cardiff area and secured some excellent gigs. The *Clubland* scene in Wales was very buoyant and lots of clubs were paying good money. I had often heard other acts talk about weekends in the area. Clubs would pay extra for performers from other parts of the country, getting special billing and promotion. I could do with the cash to fund my double life.

For the next six months, I spent every other weekend away in South Wales. The weekends that I was home, sent me into a depression. I remember one Sunday sitting all day on the floor with my back against a hot radiator in the dining room, the stereo system continuously playing those albums that reminded me of Belgium and seemed to bring her closer to me.

 I was still sharing the same bed with my wife and we would go about our daily life in a fairly normal fashion, but there was an unhealthy atmosphere. My two girls, who were at home, must have been aware of the strain. I resisted her advances in the bedroom and eventually she stopped trying. Inevitably the snide remarks began to creep in, how faithful was I being to my lover etc etc.

 Relationships between her and my parents were now preventing the children having any contact with them, if I took them thereto visit life would be hell for us all for days.

 I began to see her in a different light and it changed the way I felt for her.

As the girls got older, she got harder on them and punished them severely if they disobeyed her. She was even violent sometimes. It was never my way and it repulsed me.

It is never easy; there is never a right time, but the day came when I decided that I was going to leave home.

Red had indicated she wanted me to move in with her. It was time.

For several weeks, I planned my exit. I built a box trailer at work to go on the back of my recently acquired VW camper. It would take my motor bike and sound equipment.

Sure, I thought about my leaving lots. I hated myself because I was leaving my girls behind, although I did not see much of Karen. After she married, she had problems too, moved across town and got involved with the wrong sort. My mind was made up, though. This time I was really leaving.

I remember it was a Friday. I can't remember the exact circumstances, I have honestly blanked these few hours from my memory, but I must have taxied from the office, early in the afternoon, leaving the company car at the depot.

As I suspected, there was no one home that afternoon, only my faithful dog Danny. He greeted me, his affection for me clear to see in his body language and his eyes. I got his lead and took him for his last walk on his patch. Off we went as usual, not far but just enough distance for him to do his stuff and for us to have a bit of a play on the nearby open park area, our normal routine. Within minutes he started walking back. He dragged me back home as normal, the leather part of the lead in his mouth, me holding the clip that normally went on his collar. Role reversal! Who was in charge, me or him?

A Standard Poodle, he had been the runt of the litter, the only one left. I had been lucky to get him because he turned into the most fantastic, loyal dog, and no way was I leaving him behind.

My VW stood ready on the drive, secretly pre-packed over the last few weeks with personal belongings. I just needed to throw in my clothes. I quickly filled two black rubbish sacks and look around my house, for the last time.

This was the point of no return. I was filled with anxiety. I had experienced different emotions over the last few days, as my exit drew near. At times I felt like a bastard, my 25th wedding anniversary less than six months away. If I stayed until then, I was sure I would never leave. Yet how could I stay, feeling the way I did?

I settled Danny in and sat there for what seemed like a lifetime, memories, flashing through my mind. My fingers slowly closed over the key and twisted it. Time to go Norman.

The engine whirred, clicked and died. Fuck! The battery was flat! *Great timing!*

Sweating with nervous energy coursing through my veins, I started rolling the camper backwards down the drive. We lived on the crest of a busy road that fell away in both directions. I apply the brakes when I suddenly spotted my daughter, Samantha, walking home from college.

" Shit shit shit!. Now what?"

At nineteen. she was aware of the circumstances.

"Hi, Dad, what are you doing?"

I was honest with her.

"Sam, I am leaving, going to Wales."

Her face fell, but as we talked, she shocked me by saying,

"I don't know how you stayed so long."

She seemed to understand. I don't exactly know what was going on her mind at that point. I shrugged and shook my head. Putting my arm round her shoulders, I smiled into her eyes.

"Battery's flat. Wanna give your old man a push?"

As I drove away my eyes filled with tears, Through the rear-view mirror I could see her standing there, her slight figure watching me go, hand raised waving goodbye.

Chapter 10

I'll be there tonight

I hated myself. Unsure of the future, all I knew was that I had to keep driving. I had no intention of abandoning my children. I had not fallen out of love with them.

 I headed for the office and arrived after everyone had left. Opening the gates, I drove to the workshop, dragged my trailer out and hitched it up to the camper. Then I loaded my small motorcycle, along with other important items. All I needed now was my sound system out of the boot of my car. Danny ran around the enclosed yard, having a good sniff, as I went into the office and called Red.

"I've done it. I'm on my way."

 "I love you, see you soon. Drive safely."

Those few words were all I needed to hear.

That would be the longest, most agonising journey of my life.

'Torn between two lovers,' the song goes.

 Well, I was torn.

To make matters worse, on the way, my wife called, pleading, crying, desperate for me to change my mind and go back home. So desperate, even threatening to harm herself. It was the first time I had heard her really break down and sob so intensely. My mind was all over the place. At one point, I almost did turn around, but at the bottom of my heart I knew she would not do anything stupid.

That call was followed shortly afterwards by another. My sister in law, trying to find a way to reconcile the situation. I did feel very bad about myself, but surely she had seen this coming. The months of weekends away must have prepared her in some way, for this moment.

I hung up with renewed resolve, my pal Danny lounging contentedly beside me on the passenger seat, enjoying the quality time with me. I was glad of his company. The journey from Manchester to Swansea took around five hours on a good day. This trip, with a loaded trailer, would take twice as long.

The wintry weather as we hit the mountains in the Welsh wilderness was foul. Heavy rain with intermittent thunderstorms and hailstones. The windshield wipers worked overtime, straining to maintain visibility. The VW struggled with the trailer up through the mountain passes, but never missed a beat. Music, of course, was in good supply, via the BBC Radio 2 channel. I also had a box of personal tapes, and for once, the cassette player managed not to chew and devour any, as was the norm!

 As I hit the worst of the storm, Red called again, anxious, impatient to see me. I could hear the love in her voice.

Tired and hesitant, after driving for almost ten hours I eventually pulled up outside her house.

Rather than jumping straight out into my new life, I took a moment. I breathed a sigh of relief that the journey was over, knowing full well it was just the beginning, unsure of how this relationship was going to pan out or the consequences of leaving my wife and kids behind.

I switched off my mobile. With a gentle stroke of Danny's head, I assured him that everything would be okay, and headed up the drive to the rear door.

Red greeted me with the warmest, most welcoming bear hug. I melted into her arms. My eyes welled up with emotion, and things suddenly looked a little clearer. Danny had found a bowl of water, already set down for him in his new home and in his usual manner managed to splash the water everywhere, I apologised.

"Red, meet Danny."

Once again, her hair, her makeup, was immaculate. She looked beautiful and smelt even better.

Yes, I was definitely doing the right thing,

Lyrics to a song about the journey that day.

'I'll be there tonight'.

I would give it all up tomorrow, just to be with you,

Even tho' it would bring sorrow,

To more than just a few.

My head would be heavy my conscience, would be full,

Words don't come easy as you count the cost of love.

Keep the door open, leave on the light,

You know I am coming and I'll be there tonight.

You said you would love when the time was right,

Well, I just left a letter and I'll be there tonight.

Baby don't go to sleep, stay by the phone,

Listen for the Harley and when you here the drone,

Put on your lipstick, you know the one I like

Spray on some perfume cos I'll be there tonight.

The weeks passed swiftly. Red's family welcomed me and her two young girls loved Danny. We planned to redecorate the bedroom and I did some DIY jobs around the house, in between looking for full-time employment. I knew I couldn't continue commuting to Manchester in the week, where I stayed with my parents. This also gave me a little more time to see my children, giving me a chance to explain my actions.

Through a network of people, I got myself an interview with a large company who had a hire depot in Neath, near Swansea. I persuaded them to give me an opportunity to create business for them in the Cardiff/Bristol area, as my market research clearly showed a gap in their operations. Their business, office and container hire, was the same industry I was currently employed in. I had sowed a seed via conversations with the manager in their Manchester depot, because he knew about my success at AG, my current firm. We were competitors.

I got the job. A new challenge that came with the all-important but necessary company car, necessary because the gigs were rolling in too.
Gradually I found that long-lost spring in my step, and yes, as it happened, it was indeed spring.

A year on, I was setting up a new depot, outside Cardiff, in Newport. Part of the challenge to improve business in the area. A derelict site was fenced off and a building converted into offices and workshop for us. A new secretary, poached from another local competitor, (a good move), helped the daily hire business take off, while I planned and pursued the big bucks, units for education accommodation, i.e. temporary classrooms.

I secured an order from Cardiff council worth over £50,000.

Nobody, particularly not the guys at Neath office, had mentioned that Newport was a very depressed area, known for its drug problems. This resulted in weeks of vandalism at my new depot. Every night we would have units stripped of electrical/plumbing fittings and windows smashed. Their reaction? Shrugging shoulders and a '*Could have told you that,*' expression. It was stressing me out, but I didn't say anything to Red.

I booked a holiday for us in Portugal. I badly needed a holiday. Work, the separation, divorce and proceedings had all taken their toll. As we flew out over Wales that afternoon, I looked down and knew that on my return, I would have problems galore. I tried to block it out.

I wasn't wrong.

 Back into work and accompanying stress mode, after a two hour drive on that awful M4, that should have taken half the time, I was informed that my new secretary had resigned and there had been more vandalism. Also, a large classroom block installation was going badly wrong, Naturally, they blamed me for not being there. I set up a meeting with my local manager, Gary and the CEO, and we parted company.

Red was loving, understanding and supportive but I was in a whole lot of trouble. I had a mortgage in Manchester and had recently taken out a mortgage on Red's house, so she could pay her ex-husband off. I had taken a huge risk and now I risked losing Red as well.

Over the last few years, I had done a fair few favours for my mate, Ian. I had designed layouts for the hotel and helped with planning applications. In desperation, knowing he was buying a new hotel, I suggested Red and I ran it for him. He agreed in principal over the phone, which left the burning question:

Would Red relocate?

Chapter 11

Heartbreak Hotel

After one of her amazing curries, we sat on the sofa, arms around each other, reminiscing about our recent holiday in Cabanas, in the south of Portugal, close to the Spanish border. The place itself was okay, a mixture of old and new, a small resort in its infancy. Our complex had been almost on the beach, and you could hear the roar of the ocean from our room. It was a little outdated, but we had made the best of it and met some interesting people.

To get to the beach from the apartment, you had to take a rowing boat across an inland estuary, although at low tide you could walk across. Old men with rugged faces, wrinkled by the sun, probably fishermen in the younger days, worked these water taxis.

I had felt happy there. The sun was hot; I was with my woman. Gemma and Joanne, her girls, were growing on me (*they were around five and three then*). I felt alive, the worries about home filed away at the back of my head. We had a few boozy nights in a small bar, with some great people. Apart from our rundown complex, one other existed, a modern holiday village, which seemed to be filled with Germans.

We frequented The Piano Bar close to this new complex, the eatery and music venue. It had mainly English clients and was the only music venue in Cabanas, owned by a Brit. The place was packed every night and a steady flow of drinkers during the day. Before the end of the week, I was thinking of buying it! I had agreed a price of £80,000 with the owner, which included two apartments above the bar, which overlooked the sea. (*I wonder what it is like now twenty years on and what the value is?*).

He telephoned me on my return, trying to complete the deal, (*this was before the Lake District plan*), but that idea was a step too far. I knew that, but would have taken the risk had Red been in agreement.

Now I had a new plan and that night seemed the ideal opportunity to broach it. Although it did come with its disadvantages. It would mean moving away from her parents and sister. Having said that, there were so many positive points. We needed a fresh start as a new family. My plan was to up sticks and move to the Lake District, some five hours away, by car. A major decision, for her. The children would have to move schools, which would make things difficult with their father. Swansea was all she knew. Fortunately, she was able to see the bigger picture, and bravely and unselfishly agreed.

House prices at this time were at an all-time low, so we rented out Red's house to cover its costs, and made the move to the Lake District.

 Over the last few months, I had noticed something strange about Red's behaviour. There were times when she seemed to be far away, lost in another world. For no more than five or ten seconds, she would go quiet and stare into space, then touch her nose several times. I didn't think too much about it then, but in hindsight, maybe I should have.

The Gables Hotel, Ambleside, would be our new address, a thirteen-bedroom Victorian hotel, with large black and white gables! Overlooking the central park area and next to the church, the location was excellent and we were soon in at the deep end.

The Lakes were always busy. Previously the hotel had been run by a local family for over thirty years. It was a little dated, but they had clients who came every year, so we would have to change things gradually.

We had separate accommodation, an annexe attached to the main building, with two bedrooms and our own lounge. I took on the role of cook. On average, twenty breakfasts to prepare daily, but it didn't stop there. I had to meet and greet, answer the telephone, clean rooms and do some daily DIY, as there was always something falling off somewhere, especially in the shower cubicles. Red meanwhile, shared the cleaning of the rooms and her main job, apart from being my number one waitress, was the laundry.

The girls' school was a literally a stone's throw away, so that was a real plus. Danny soon found his place on an easy chair in reception. He had probably worked out that we passed through there several times an hour so he had contact with us and he was there, to do his share of the meeting and greeting.

Running a hotel is hard work, you will either get to love it or hate it. I loved it, welcoming people and making them feel at home, not unlike the entertainment game.

We soon had our accommodation looking and feeling like home, and the first mad, hectic part of the season was over. It slowed down a little in mid-October. We had been full on for five months. I had come through it and loved it. I even found time to do at least one gig a week, Saturdays mainly, after we had checked all our guests in.

Red was exhausted by this time. The last few months had taken their toll. She missed her family, and was looking forward to her mother coming to visit.

The girls had settled into school and had made lots of new friends. Ian and his wife Helen were a five-minute walk away, so support was always there, even though they were running an even larger guest house.

Red's family came to visit and had a lovely time. Tears all round on their last day, leaving Red, feeling lonely and homesick. I was lucky in that respect. My parents and children only lived about two hours away, so I saw quite a lot of them.

Ian came around for his weekly chinwag.

"How do you fancy a trip to London?" was his parting line, as he headed out the door.

"Cliff's in concert at Wembley. You'd better say yes, it's all booked."

The door closed behind him

A beaming smile spread across Red's face. I had forgotten how beautiful she was; I hadn't seen her smile like that for a while. I was happy too, it would be good for us to get away for the weekend. I had been getting out to go to gigs, in Carlisle, Kendal, Whitehaven and I had started fell-walking with Danny. Red had been tied too long to The Gables. The concert would do us good.

Ian's car was loaded with our cases for our weekend away in London, the girls had a sitter, Carole, a good friend, who also agreed to take care of the hotel.

Ian got a good deal for rooms at the Wembley Hilton. We arrived one night before the concert which gave us time to do a little sightseeing.

As we left the Hilton on the way to the concert, we asked the concierge at the main desk if he could recommend a good restaurant within walking distance of the hotel and venue where we could eat after the show. He suggested a Chinese and we asked him to book a table for us at 10.30pm.

Cliff, as usual, was fantastic. A great showman with a superb band, playing over two hours of hits plus a good selection of new songs.

His new songs were of particular interest to me, to include in my repertoire later down the line. We were standing up, out of our seats, dancing and singing along with him and the 50,000 other mad fans. It was exilerating and exhausting.

It took some time to exit the stadium. The stroll in the winter air to the restaurant was refreshing. On arrival at the restaurant, the door was closed, the blinds down. We knocked and eventually were allowed in. It was a typical Chinese restaurant, high-gloss varnish, gilt furniture and lots of red velvet, yet with an edge over the standard Chinese. The first to arrive, we were seated between two large tables, one round, one rectangular, both reserved. .

As the night unfolded, members of the Conservative party arrived and sat at the round table. Thirteen places, one with a teddy bear! We recognised the faces and we had a competition to see who we could name.

I still have a newspaper clipping, from The Manchester News, an interview I had, from that night.

"The Pekinese Restaurant, Wembley, in the company of Norma Major, Tim Rice, and Michael Barrymore." Not on the same table I might add!

The night began to warm up, and soon the atmosphere was vibrant. Red and I had our backs to the other table and the entrance.

"Guess who's just walked in?" Ian raised his eyebrows, waiting for me to guess.

"John Major?"

"Don't look round. It's Cliff!"

OMG! It took every ounce of willpower not to swivel round, but I resisted.

The atmosphere suddenly shot up a few notches, as Cliff's party of six sat down at the other table. The man himself was literally sitting back to back with me. After all, those years of listening to him on a record, there he was at arm's length. I couldn't believe our luck.

"When I tell my sister she will be so jealous. She is a real fan," gushed Red.

Ian, in his usual laid-back style didn't make a fuss, while his wife Helen, was sitting goggle-eyed, taking it all in, in prize position, facing their table. We had finished our food, so we ordered another bottle of wine and continued talking, quietly. The wine flowed, and Cliff's party still hadn't finished their meal, so we ordered another bottle.

We spent a fortune on wine that night, but it was worth it as we eventually plucked up the courage to introduce ourselves. Cliff was most gracious and introduced me to Bill Latham, his religious mentor.

Cliff told me how much he loved the Everly Brothers and that he was doing some recording with Phil Everly. I must have mentioned something to spark the conversation off, as I too was an Everly fan. At this point, we sang the first couple of verses of Dream together. He stopped, saying he had to rest his voice, understandably. He had weeks of concerts ahead of him.

We continued talking. I worked him into a corner for a few minutes and had him all to myself. I explained I had some songs most suitable for his voice and he agreed to listen to them. He told me to come to the Sheffield concert, in a few weeks and bring the tapes. Sheffield was the next venue nearest to our Lakes location. He said our names would be on the door. We gave our details to Bill.

I introduced Red to Cliff, explaining how we had met and then we posed for a photograph, kindly taken by one of the Chinese waiters.

Cliff held Red tightly around her waist, I was shoulders on to Cliff and Bill had his arm on my other shoulder. Then he wrote on our concert programme,

'To Red and Norman, It's all my fault,' Cliff Richard.

I remember then standing outside with Cliff, still talking about music. He was wearing a light checked jacket with blue jeans and he kept adjusting his long woollen scarf, protecting his throat from the chill of the night air. We shook hands, he kissed Red on the cheek and we went our separate ways.

How much of a 'One Fine Day' was that?

Some weeks later I was in Sheffield. Would this be another *if only* moment? It was a spectacular amazing arena, and once again, the show was brilliant. At halftime I went to the stage door and sure enough my name was on the guest list. I left a tape with two new songs with one of Cliff's entourage.

" Look here, this is a tape for Cliff. He is expecting it, it has two new songs for him," I expressed. I didn't want to disturb him.

"Make sure he gets it."

Then I left. Trying not to be pushy or forceful, I thought that was the right thing to do. But was it? Did he get the tape? Who knows?

I never had any further communication.

It was Carnival week. Situated at the top end of Windermere, Ambleside was a great central location, a tourist magnet, and the Gables was full.

Thirty people in a walking party had already been staying for three of four nights. Each morning they would filter in for breakfast in twos and threes.

The previous night had been a very late one, considering we were normally in bed by eleven. I overslept and woke up late, realising I had forgotten to prepare the bacon and mushrooms the night before.

I ran down the back stairs to the kitchen, hair brush in hand. I opened the fire door from the kitchen to the dining room to see thirty-two people waiting for their breakfast! We had had some fun over the last few days, so fortunately, because of my sense of humour, we were able to laugh about it.

Within an hour I managed to knock up sixty-four eggs, cooked to perfection, with bacon, served by Red with a red-lipped smile. They were then ready to walk the wonderful fells of the Lake District, leaving me without egg on my face!

I wrote this song around that time:

Girl I love you

I'm falling in love with you again
Even though we never fell out,
I'm loving you much more each day
Hoping I don't burn out.

Your fuelling my fire with your touch,
You're burning me up inside
I still can't believe I am here with you
I wake up, you're by my side,

I kiss your face as the sun comes up
Your lips as the sun goes down,
My days are filled with happiness
Just knowing that you're around.

Girl, I love you, I can't stop saying
That I love you,
And if I'm boring with I love you
Then I adore you so much.

Only a few weeks later, I had another late night. I had been in Carlisle, working in a club. At that time, I had a Ford Escort estate, bought before we left Swansea. A good reliable family car and excellent for carrying my sound equipment.

It was towards the end of October, a wet and windy night. I suppose I was tired as I drove home. The roads were covered with falling leaves from the Lakeland trees as I wove my way through the mountain roads, anxious to get back to The Gables.

Suddenly, I lost the back end of the car! Sideways, I could see a wooden fence and a copse of trees coming towards me. I closed my eyes as the car slid off the road, crashed through the fence and descended down a steep bank.

With my eyes still shut, I waited until the noise of door panels bouncing off the trees and the tinkling of breaking glass, stopped. When I opened my eyes, it was pitch black. My first instinct was to try to restart the car, and as ever she fired up. I slipped her into gear, the engine revved, I let out the clutch and the wheels just spun around.

We were going nowhere. I switched the engine off and slowly checked myself over. Legs, arms, my head, everything seemed okay. Fuck, that was a lucky one!

Shit, I thought. What about my PA system?

I carefully opened my door and stared down in horror. The car was in a stream! Every panel I could see was damaged. The rear nearside door was bent double and several windows were smashed.

I must have shut the worst of it out because, I don't retain an image of the car sitting on that river bed.

I must have got the hatchback open because I scrambled to the road, up the soaked bank, avoiding sections of broken fence and strips of entwined barbed wire, several times, piling my amp, speakers, briefcase, and clothes bag up on the side of the desolate mountain road. I stood there in a daze hoping to see a pair of headlights coming my way. I don't remember looking back down the bank.

Then it came to me in a flash. I had lost control when a car, speeding, had blinded me with its headlights, and I misjudged the bend.

As if by magic, a Volvo estate came to a halt just minutes after I sat on my gear at the side of the road. By now I was cold and feeling a bit of a numpty. A kind man loaded me and my gear into his car and took me to his home in Keswick. We had some tea as he arranged a taxi for me, to take me back to Ambleside. A true gentleman and my saviour.

I paid the taxi driver out of my earnings that night, and noticed the clock on his dashboard said 3.15 am. I stood outside the hotel for a few minutes looking at the full moon in all its glory, casting shadows of the trees across the glistening bowling green. Then I took a deep breath as I entered the rear door and climbed the stairs to our bedroom in the annexe, where I found Red in a deep sleep. She had not been well that day. She had had one of those strange quiet moments, followed by a migraine. I slipped under the sheets, hoping for a few hours sleep before I had to prepare breakfast.

I awoke just before the alarm was due to start its unharmonious beeping. I kissed Red on the cheek and went downstairs to prepare breakfast, fortunately only for around twelve people.

Only after the dishwasher was on, tables cleared and reset for the following morning, did I ask her to sit down. I told her about the previous night's events.

I was expecting her to be angry; she was always telling me I did too much should be taking things easier. She just looked at me and burst into tears, grateful I was still in one piece.

For me autumn is a poignant time of the year, the end of the long summer days and the beginning of those long dark afternoons. The landscape loses its green camouflage and the trees take on a plethora of colours. Walking through Rothay Park at the side of the hotel with Red one afternoon, looking at the autumnal landscape, inspired this song:

RED

I call her Red

Even though she didn't like the phrase

I call her Red,

her hair shines through the autumn haze.

She is my girl a woman and a friend

And I pray to God our love will never end.

If I told you that we hardly ever meet

Would you think it strange our love is so strong?

You and I have a love that is complete

And it grows each day that we are apart.

In January, the hotel trade was at its quietest. Most hoteliers went on holiday just after New Year. The previous year we had been to Tenerife with Ian and Helen. That year we drove up to Scotland in our newly acquired bright Red Mitsubishi 4x4. We had rented a log cabin in a ski resort near Aviemore. We didn't intend to ski, just enjoy a break and explore the area.

Actually, it was good for us all. We relaxed, had fun, laughed a lot and de-stressed. We had great fun driving through the snow in our new car. I had never actually had an off-road car before. It was a good experience, and perfect for the Lakes.

One night, while sharing a bottle of sparkling wine in our cosy log cabin, Red and I talked about how our lives were going. It had not been a smooth ride so far and wasn't going as planned either. We were now in our fourth year together. It was clear she missed her family and she said she wasn't looking forward to another long season at The Gables.

I loved her and didn't want to lose her. What could I do?

I, on the other hand, loved the Lakes. Although cold and wet most of the time, the air was fresh and my asthma was under control. My music was in decline because of the workload, but I was content enough. Wales was not good for my health, that was for sure. I had been hospitalised twice whilst working there.

When we returned after our lovely winter holiday, I spoke to Ian, who had just returned from his timeshare in Tenerife. I explained my dilemma. A lifelong friend, I had to be straight with him, to give him time to find someone to take over The Gables

What I didn't expect was for things to make an about-turn so abruptly. Just one phone call, shortly after speaking to Ian, an ex-colleague gave me a contact number for a company in Oxford, which led to me being offered a job in Devon.

Saying goodbye to Ian and Helen was difficult, but they say things happen for a reason. Our decision had been made. Onwards and upwards.

From the left: Yours truly, Bill Latham, Red, Sir Cliff.

Spring again, time for a change, especially in my case and right on cue, we were about to depart from our life in Ambleside. It was 1995.

When we moved from Swansea, my daughter Sam and her boyfriend, Keith, had helped us. We hired a 7.5-ton van, and we used their services again to relocate to Devon. This time Keith provided us with a small caravan, which we towed behind the 4x4. This would be our temporary accommodation while we found our feet in Devon. Keith drove the truck, and in convoy we steadily absorbed the miles.

We were heading for Bovey Tacey, a town near Torquay. The job was the same industry I had been in for several years before the hotel.

Red was very happy, as our new location was less than three hours from Swansea and she could see her folks on a more regular basis.

I had been to the office in Oxford before, with the MD after my interview, so I had met the staff and was looking forward to another challenge, as once again, there were problems. The current manager, Wolfgang, a German guy, although good at his job, was not well-liked by the company, displaying too many Germanic ways, unable to completely adapt to the UK.

One of his achievements however, impressed me. He had won a contract to supply all the temporary units for *The Glastonbury Festival.* This involved stage dressing rooms, first aid, booking offices and of course toilets, hundreds of them.

My first priority however, was to find a place for our caravan. Storage for our furniture and belongings was not a problem, as we had a yard full of containers and I had the key to the yard, so when we arrived on Sunday morning, we unloaded everything there. We had a short drive then to a holiday park less than a mile away, where we set up camp, eager for our new adventure.

 We had something to eat together before Sam and Keith left to go back to Manchester with the hire truck, and we prepared for our first night in our supposedly four-berth caravan. It was cramped but fun and would be our home for a month at least. The camp, (closed for many years now), was part of The Trago Mills company, a large retail store and visitor's attraction. There was an indoor heated swimming pool that we could use anytime and a play park nearby. What could be better?

The next day, we all drove into the office, where I introduced Red and the kids to my new office staff. Red then left in the 4x4 to look around and see what schools were on offer. Bev, my new secretary, had given Red some papers and directions. I settled in, re-arranged my office and tried to get rid of the smell of stale cigarettes. Wolfgang had been a heavy smoker.

It is not long before we found a house to rent in Chudleigh, Knighton, just minutes away from the office. A two-bedroom, cottage style home with a small garden, with an open aspect to the front and two pubs and a school less than a five-minute walk away.

In my usual way, I soon made friends, had the depot and staff reorganised and things were going well. My first Glastonbury Festival has been and gone, enjoyable but a logistic nightmare. Transporting fifty to sixty container-type buildings to the festival site, some 32ft long and driving across fields, which during the normal year were grazed by cattle, owned by the Michael Eavis family at Worthy Farm, Pilton.

The deliveries were okay, scheduled over a period of a few weeks but it rained intensely during the festival so the fields were a quagmire. I got on well with the team there and we won the contract for the following year.

During parents evening at the local school, I noticed a poster wanting people to join a male Barbershop choir, Escapela. At this point, I wasn't doing any gigs and needed some contacts, so I gave them a call. They actually rehearsed in the school, so a short walk the following Wednesday evening was the start of many new friendships with guys of all ages and from many walks of life. Two local guys, a teacher and another retired professional had started the choir, but many of the twenty or so regular members had relocated from various locations around the UK. Over the next three years we attended many events and Escapela enjoyed significant success.

We did have some breakaway groups, like Fourplay, a group I organised. Colin 1, one of the youngest of the choir members, played guitar and sang baritone. Colin 2, also in his thirties, was a tenor and Nigel, a local teacher, was a very deep baritone. I was lead singer, and together we made a great new, exciting sound. Colin and I also went out and worked some holiday camps as The Bovey Boys, taking the name from a local village we both frequented.

Red had worked for Barclays Bank for the last couple of years and the girls were growing up fast. We had already moved to a slightly larger house which we had on a mortgage, still only with two bedrooms, when we really needed three.

Red's 'moments' returned, only this time, on a much more regular basis, so that it interfered with her life. She sought medical help and was diagnosed with epilepsy. This put pressure on our relationship, which was sliding downhill fast. Socialising went out the window, as she felt under the weather most of the time. When she felt she could cope, she would be working or running the girls to different places.

Financial pressures didn't help either. We were struggling to pay our existing mortgage, while still on the lookout for a three-bed property. With prices rising fast, things were becoming impossible.

I decided to put our house on the market, and unbelievably, it sold in two days! Now we had a real dilemma, forced into decisions before we were ready to make them.

The outcome was, unfortunately, to separate. Red rented a two-bed house for her and the children. I had just turned fifty and feeling very confused and disillusioned. I needed an economical solution, so a mobile home seemed to be the answer.

The sale of our home gave us a little profit, which gave us financial independence at least and as the sale was finalised, I bought a property, of sorts. I found an old caravan! Classed as a mobile home with an asking price of £9000.

And so we come full circle to the beginning of my story.

I had no choice but to live in it while doing it up. It was a bit of a building site, but every day a little bit more got done, before and after my day at the office.

Eventually, the old porch had gone, a new side pod was added, which included part of the new kitchen and breakfast bar. A new extra-wide entrance door completed the new look, along with new cladding over the existing aluminium corrugated panels, (*standard on most caravans*), and a new pitched roof finished the job off.

 That particular evening, I was walking the dog. The residents of the caravan park, mostly retired, were taking advantage of the mild, warm evening to water their plants or mow the lawn. A few raised their hand in greeting, others muttered hello as we passed by.

There was one old van on an untidy plot, shaded by a huge poplar tree full of roosting crows. It had a bit of a reputation for being noisy. Some nights the noise just before dusk was enough to wake the dead. With the TV on constantly and the volume maxed out, he had to be as deaf as a post. At least the noise of the crows wouldn't bother him, that's for sure. The windows were never open and condensation ran down the single-glazed aluminium frames. I had often wondered, over the last four months, who lived there.

I reckoned I had to be the youngest person on the park. For most it was their last stop. Mind you, I had felt that way too a couple of months ago. Fifty and finished, a complete failure at life.

I walked past Jack's van, actually, a mobile home of sorts. A few decades old, but certainly no caravan. He had moved in shortly after me with his missus. He told me he had been a driving instructor most of his life, then a heart attack and triple bypass had put an end to his career at fifty-five. A heavy smoker and a chap who liked a drink. We used to walk over to the local football club several nights a week for a game of pool (*he always won*), and a few pints. Jack had also helped me with the final part of the roof.

I usually saw him on our doggy walk, but that night he wasn't there.

The next caravan, on a very tidy plot, belonged to a German lady in her seventies called Crystal. She was out in the garden, watering. I could see her hip was giving her trouble.

"Hello young man, would you like a cup of tea? It's a lovely evening to sit in the garden."

"Thank you, tea would be lovely."

She told me she was an artist, a member of the local guild of painters and played the organ for the local church.

We chatted for quite some time. Softly-spoken, she looked directly into my eyes. We discovered that we had things in common and her accent reminded me of Helena. Her pale skin looked soft, younger than her age. I sensed an almost subconscious attraction for her and that the feeling was mutual!

Over the following weeks, we got to know each other better. She often cooked lunch, I showed her how to enjoy her music more, by adding a small amplifier and headphones to her very dated electric organ, allowing her to play it louder without disturbing the neighbours. I invited her to listen to some of my songs back at my place. The interior had been finished and we enjoyed each other's company.

Red came over to visit. I invited her the first time, and everything went smoothly. I didn't make a move on her, and she returned several times, just for a meal. Gradually, friendship established itself as the forerunner over passion in the relationship. It was obvious that we both cared about one other. For my part, my feelings still ran deep, but there was a distance between us, an invisible line I was reluctant to cross, knowing if I pushed things, I could lose everything. The children also paid me a visit, and my parents came and stayed for several weeks. With harmony in the ranks, I certainly didn't want to ruin any of that, just for lack of female company.

After living in what seemed like Beirut for months, I could finally put hand on heart and say the old van had undergone a complete transformation, from van to mobile home. Crystal wasn't the only one who wanted to see the inside. The whole neighbourhood it seemed, were curious. Well, it was one way of making friends I suppose.

My last small job was the bottom skirting with a band of plywood panels. The table saw was out again and I was making quite a bit of a noise. The usually quiet retirement park had suffered a fair amount of disruption after my descent into their chosen piece of paradise. I bashed, banged and sang my way heedlessly through many a weekend and evening, invading their nightly episodes of Coronation Street and Emmerdale, with the obvious ensuing disgruntled reactions.

That day, the tall blonde from next door came up my drive to complain about the noise. I explained that I was trying my best to make as little noise as possible. She was dressed very smartly, even had some makeup on and her face looked fresh. As she spoke, her eyes transfixed on mine, she edged nearer to the new main door to catch a glimpse inside. Her eyes locked on mine, unblinking. She stopped talking. I instinctively dried up, not wanting to blink first, my eyes beginning to smart and sting with the effort. She was trying to seduce me!

Hell no! Yes, I wanted the attention of a woman but if Crystal and the tall blonde from next door were the only prospective candidates, then I would have to respectfully decline. No, no, no, they did not exactly fit the bill. Not at all. I was used to younger women.

Ian would laugh and quote:

'Many an old tune played on an old fiddle.'

That tune was not for me. Not yet.

The lyrics to a new song, written around this insecure period:

I'm still confused

I'm still confused, still looking for the truth, and who am I?

And why have I done all the foolish things in my life?

Chasing a dream, it's greener on the other side,

And maybe, this time, I will find my peace of mind.

Chase a dream, leaving you behind, running away,

Someone else is on my mind.

Chase a dream, break another heart,

Leave everything behind, only to find,

The weakness was in my mind.

Thought I could make it girl, wanted to change the world,

I never wanted to turn it upside down.

It was summertime, a great time to be in Devon. That weekend I had a great outdoor gig, so I had invited a few friends down to support me.

Working in the office, Julie, the cleaner, popped her head through the door.

"Tea?"

"Yes, always,"

Moments later she was back with my cuppa.

"What's this gig at the weekend? You taking me?" And skipped out of the office.

This was a surprise, a lovely one. I imagined having my wicked way with her. Holding my cup, I entered the main office. Julie was sitting with Bev, my lovely secretary, and best mate. She looked up at me expectantly.

"Bev just said she is going with Wayne, (her new boyfriend), so what time shall I come round to you on Saturday?"

What could I say? She had it all worked out. Like a lamb to the slaughter...

"Make it around half-past six."

With a beaming smile, she took the empty cup from me into the kitchen, washed it up and skipped out the door. Bev was also grinning from cheek to cheek.

" What's *that* all about?"

 With an equally broad smile, I replied,

"It means I might get lucky."

Bev, never Beverly, was a natural blonde, mid-forties and my rock. I would have been lost without her. We had worked together for five years, grown very close and trusted one another with our innermost secrets. Mutual respect, often undervalued, is the hallmark of a genuine relationship, and not to be taken lightly. I often used to pass by her as she was on the phone, lift her long hair and kiss the back of her neck. It always made her squirm. But that was as far as it got. Her mum, God bless her, was always trying to get us together, but our relationship was solid, with different boundaries.

Since those days, I have spent more time out socialising with her and her friends, sometimes in real, drunken stupors after a night out in the village and in Torquay.

It was on one such occasion that Bev met Wayne, her boyfriend. I had purchased a motorhome and one night, was parked in a friend's scrap yard, near Dawlish after a 'Vicars & Tarts' night. There were three of us, me and two women. One in my bed, the other behind the curtains on the upper bunk, I was hoping for a bunk up too!

The evening had started with me dressed in a long overcoat, dragging three women behind me, on a chain wrapped around their waists. As we burst into the local pub, one we had never frequented before, it turned out we were the only ones in fancy dress! So you can imagine the reception we got! We all got extremely drunk and it was there that Bev met Wayne.

That night Jack phoned me.

"Fancy a drink, boy? I'm curmin ta pick you up," in his Devonshire drole.

Within minutes he was at my door.

"What's the rush buddy? I only just finished cooking," said I, as he walked in and slowly sat himself down, mumbling and grumbling as he did so.

"Legs playing you up?"

"Yes boy."

I sat down and started eating. He looked across at me and said, all in the same breath,

"I am going down Plymouth to see Jed. Do you want me to feed the dog?"

 He could see Danny's food unopened next to his dish.

"Great, is that Jed from the Westerners?" I said, with a mouthful of food.

"Yeah, we gort a big meetin coming up."

The Westerners were a group of people who dressed up in traditional American Cowboy, Indian and military costumes to re-enact the days of the early settlers in America.

For many years, a large private landowner, who ran The Shire Horse Centre in Devon, had allowed the group to build a typical American mid-west town film set, so they could have several meetings a year in an authentic setting. These meets could be up to two weeks in the summer and they would play out gun fights for the visitors, who came to the vast horse sanctuary and woodlands.

Typically, they would pitch traditional, white, authentic, canvas tents and even have wigwams. He told me this venue had been bought by a commercial business and they had closed the Shire Horse Centre down to develop the estate. People used to come every year from all over the country. It was a big society.

We arrived at the social club in Plymouth, a thirty-minute drive from our village. A few guys were dressed in their gear, toting pistols. Very bizarre.

A theme park in Exeter let them have their meeting there, the first meeting for two years since the closure of the horse sanctuary.

I had a drink and listened while they made a list of everything they needed to discuss with the owners of the new venue. I was introduced to a few people before we left with an official invite to the September event.

Chapter 13

A Saturday night performance

Saturday arrived. Julie turned up in her little car on time and parked outside. Curtains twitched predictably, as she walked up the drive, in slacks with trainers and a funky-looking T-shirt.

She was lively and a little loud, as usual.

"This is nice, boss," she said as she wandered around my new open-plan hall, kitchen, and lounge. "Very nice."

"Thanks," I said and then, "Okay, let's rock and roll."

We were only going down to Torquay, about fifteen miles away.

The hotel had a large terrace and the weather was perfect, for once. The Bovey boys would be doing two one-hour sets.

There was good crowd, lots of holiday makers and around ten of my friends. Our music was a mix of 60s to 80s, popular across the ages, and recently Colin had been playing a couple of instrumentals. I loved my sound effects. Every so often you would hear a gunshot, or a train going by. Best of all though, was the helicopter that seemed to fly overhead. It was a bit of fun and provided great links for a couple of jokes. We had had a hilarious evening the previous week that finished with Colin and the pub landlord, both pie-eyed, singing us out with '*Always look on the bright side of life*'.

During the interval, Bev and I introduced Julie to a few people and I got a chance to have a drink, I limited myself to one alcoholic drink when performing. Julie and the gang had already had several, over the three-hour period.

The second half was lively up-tempo songs, lots of people up dancing. After an encore or two, we finally took our well-earned applause. I grabbed a towel, wiped my face down, changed my shirt, then relaxed as the guys finished their drinks. The evening air was pleasant, a soft onshore breeze cooling us as we packed the gear away in the car. We were soon on our way back home.

"That was fantastic, boss, I never knew you could sing like that," said Julie.

Back home, I parked on the drive. Julie put her hand on my knee.

"Do you have any gin?"

I nodded.

I opened the windows, closed the blinds to block out the light to the outside and put the music on low.

Julie was rolling a joint.

 "That's a sofa bed, isn't it?"

"Yes Julie, you just pull it."

Already made up, she obediently pulled it out as I handed her a drink.

"Gin with ice and a slice."

"Cheers boss. Can I smoke?"

I opened the old double doors.

"Sure."

She made herself at home and lit up.

"Turn the music up and join me,"

"Just a bit then. Mustn't disturb the neighbours"

As I took the joint from her, she removed her blouse and slacks and sat facing me, cross-legged and we talked. About our lives, our past, mistakes, our hopes.

"Will that music go any louder?"

She jumped up and pushed the volume right up .

"Julie, the neighbours."

"Fuck the neighbours!"

I got up and pushed the volume down a notch. She frowned, had a drink and another drag on the spliff. My trousers now removed along with my shirt, we sat face to face, relaxing as the cannabis took effect. I must admit I was feeling a little out of my comfort zone, as Julie could be a little wild, but I could see she was mellowing. The loud music didn't seem to bother me any more either. I began to see her face changing shape, the spliff affecting my senses, she was becoming more beautiful, her skin seemed to be remoulding itself. I saw the face of Red.

Julie removed her bra, to reveal beautiful, small, perfectly-formed breasts and pale, flawless, smooth skin.

With a last draw on the spliff, she got up, walked across to the kitchen, threw it in the bin, turned and walked slowly and meaningfully back, simultaneously flicking off her knickers and the volume button up again, before lying stretched out on her back seductively, arms above her head.

Humming along to the music, her head tossing slowly from side to side, I was now extremely aroused and getting restless. I reached for her breast, my finger made contact.

"Oh no, not yet don't, wait", firmly removing my impatient hand.

A few minutes later, finding it hard to resist for another moment, I put my hand on her thigh, moving it tentatively in the direction of her pubic region. "I'm not ready." This time her voice was soft and slow. "I'm not ready." The wait was most rewarding.

Monday at the office started as normal. We got the transport sorted for the day then it was time for a morning cuppa.

Julie was in the office and we talked generally about the weekend and the gig. Anything else was not referred to. I was pleased about that and it remained that way.

Something inside me was telling me to get myself sorted. I was restless. It's nice to have women inviting themselves into my life and my bed, but if I was to find happiness and a decent, lasting relationship, then I would have to be proactive, get out there and find it myself. On my terms.

Therefore, a few weeks later, I made plans to take the motorhome to Spain for a break.

I booked the ferry from Plymouth to Santander and my adventure began. I drove east to Barcelona, then inland to Tarragona, down the coast to Benidorm and back through central Spain, stopping at Burgos. There, I fell in love with a property for sale in a mountain village, on the outskirts of the city. I was seduced by the whole package, the sunshine, the light, the fresh air and in that fleeting moment, considered actually moving to Spain.

The asking price was only 38.000 euros. The thought had been fleeting, however. Of course I didn't pursue it.

Around the same time, I befriended a DJ on South Hams Radio and interacted with several people on the phone-in, on his daily breakfast show.

He was also an agent specialising in Caribbean cruises and I was soon scheduled to go on a cruise with him, with other radio people and a host of locals. Maybe I would meet someone interesting onboard.

One thing the cruise gave me was a boost in my confidence, at a time when I was feeling a little insecure. Dressing up in your best refinery makes you feel good. In fact, he whole experience was confidence-building for me. The atmosphere was wonderful and the ship's crew made you feel special.

We flew to Miami, boarded the cruise liner and visited the island of Cozumel, off Mexico, Jamaica etc., and then spent some time on the Florida Quays. Ten days of fun. I joined in with lots of events. We did some karaoke nights too. Boy, did we eat, seventeen meals a day if you wanted. I did have several offers from some American women, and one in particular who looked like Lisa Minelli. She was about my age, lived in New York and was on board with her family. They said they were willing to sponsor me for a visa, think they were desperate to get her hitched.

I also got to perform in the theatre on board and was received well, even given details from one of the gang of how to apply to join Celebrity Cruises. I got a real bug for radio around this time.

I had thought about radio before and had a short spell working unofficially for the BBC in Manchester when I did the karaoke show.

The highlife behind me, no more than a month later, during a yard stock check at the depot, one of our haulage contractors drove in to collect a unit.

"Morning Ken, you look tanned,"

"Morrin, Norrman," another west country local.

He explained he had just come back from Spain, where he had bought twenty acres of land. My ears pricked up and twenty or more questions were thrown at him. It was an area not far from Barcelona that I myself had recently passed through. He had his own business, buying and selling static caravans and his idea was to set up a holiday/residential park on his Spanish plot by the river and go into retirement. I thought this was a great idea and an option for me.

For many years at the back of my mind, I had harboured thoughts of moving abroad, if nothing else for my health and well-being, which flourish in a warmer climate. Flights from our local airport were reasonable, so within a few weeks I went to visit his new home to be.

I was there for two days and loved it so much that I bought a plot of land myself. Just two acres, but with planning permission to build a small house. The best £15,000 I ever spent. The plot was two kilometres out of the village, five minutes in the car, up a dirt track more suitable for a 4x4.

The area was called Baixantees which means 'all roads lead down'. It was a flat strip of land, around fifty metres wide, which had been planted with cherry trees of which only one remained, almost dead centre of the plot. At the far end away from the track was a shaded area with a copse of old pine trees.

There was a higher terrace behind me and a lower one beneath, giving an unrestricted view down to the village and across the valley to the mountains some sixty kilometres away.

Ginestar, was the small village that I looked down on, my village. It had a population of around five hundred, situated in the Ebro Valley, with mountain views in every direction and the magnificent River Ebro, winding its way through the valley. It was a great location.

The Ebro is the longest river in Spain at 910 kilometres long. It starts way up in the north around Santander, ending in the Mediterranean, after negotiating the marshlands of the Ebro Delta National Park, the most significant wetland in Europe.

On the opposite side of the river was another village, Miravet, famous for the last battle of the Spanish civil war in 1938, known as the Battle of the Ebro. High above the village, a magnificent Templar castle looks down over the river and it is the most well-preserved in Europe.

Chapter 14

Home is where you park it

I had a very unexpected phone call from Gemma, Red's eldest daughter, saying she didn't know what to do. Her mum had been taken into hospital. I went as quickly as I could and met them there. Red had suffered a massive epileptic fit. The girls, Gemma and Joanne, had been with her when it happened and called an ambulance. They were in shock. I had been like a father to them for the last six years, so I was the obvious person to ring and I was so pleased they did.

I looked at Red, as she lay recovering. I took her hand and tears filled my eyes, as all my feelings for her, so long repressed, came flooding back. I made the decision there and then that I would try to get our relationship back on track, that perhaps it was meant to be. After all, I saw Red and the girls every few weeks, we had never cut the cord, so the transition wouldn't be so difficult.

The following day Red was given the all clear. I went with the girls to collect her. They had not gone to school, as they had been staying with me at my place. We went back to the little rented house where they had been for the last year. That night I stayed in her bed. We were together once again.

The following day, her mother and father travelled from Wales to spend some time with her so, after a brief reunion with them I went to work, and that night I slept back at my place.

The house that they were renting was actually up for sale, so they were facing the prospect of having to move out. Maybe this added pressure had caused her attack. I contacted the agent and made an offer. The market was in recession at this point, and they accepted. I had the deposit and knew a good a good broker, so in a matter of weeks we owned the house. Now that we had a semblance of security, things were looking up and I was soon spending more time with her and the girls than I was at my own home.

I did have another important decision to make around this point in my life. Danny, now in his seventeenth year, was fading fast, I had to think about saying goodbye to my faithful friend. I took him round to Indiopond, a local fishery, where there was a grooming parlour. Danny went every six or seven weeks and I wanted to see him looking his best. I explained to the lady who groomed him that it would be for the last time.

That weekend I took him to Manchester, to see my girls, staying at my parents as usual. It was a sad time. My ex-wife sent a message via my daughter, saying she would like to see him. It had been, more than twelve years since we had left home, but he remembered her and seemed so happy to see her. I was amazed at his reaction. The following week, he was at rest. I knew it was the right thing to do.

My little mobile home suddenly seemed much bigger and very empty. Over the two short years I had been there, I had managed to amass so many memories. The reform, the curtain twitchers, John the milkman, Jack, Crystal. The time my parents had stayed - even my girls had been down, all of them at different times, plus my own enjoyable evenings!

I had paid £9000 for it and around £3000 to refurbish, using my own labour, and buying materials all at trade prices, making it an economical project. It sold for £50,000 within the month, even though the market was quiet.

It soon became clear that this small house we had bought was just that. Small. Not big enough for us all. We had landed ourselves in the exact same position as before. The girls needed their own space. We eventually gave in and rented a new townhouse in Bovey Tracey. It had three large bedrooms plus an extra small room, to use as a study as by then we had a home computer.

The year was 2003. We let the other house, which covered some of the costs towards the bigger home, but we still had a huge increase in our monthly outgoings. I seemed to be working just to meet our commitments. I wasn't doing any gigs and I had given up the Barbershop choir. I was happy to be back with Red but nothing was quite the same and her illness was gradually getting worse. We had a lot of stress. Gemma was causing us a few problems with boys and Joanne was having regular sessions with a psychiatrist, regarding her increasing eating disorder and the development of obsessive-compulsive disorder. This had been in evidence since she was about five years old. Who knows about these things? But I am convinced it was triggered by the marriage breakup. With Gemma, it was just her hormones.

I had been able to continue my project in Spain, allowing me some relief from our family troubles. I installed a large static caravan on my land, purchased from Ken, dug a septic tank,
installed a water collection system and bought a generator. Then started the main build, a small house, with the help of two of my ex-brother in laws! Yes, it's true, they held nothing against me.

Tony, was a builder in semi-retirement, who drove over to Spain in his van, with Mike, who had also been retired in his forties with white finger, caused by excessive vibration, he had been a tree surgeon.

The van arrived loaded with scaffolding, a cement mixer, spades and a variety of power tools. They stayed for over six weeks. I had ten days and two full weekends, and within that time we managed to put up the shell of a house and install the roof beams. Red and the girls came out and helped during this period. We had a great time, blue skies and long sunny days. Gemma and Joanne learning how to use a trowel, with guidance from Tony and Mike. They pointed the joints between the brickwork, while getting a tan.

They complained too because they could not use their hairdryers and hair straighteners unless the generator was running, and even then only one appliance at a time. It was another way of existence, basically camping.

Recording in Devon

I could feel a creative period coming on, for some time. I had an urge to write a couple of songs, and armed with this thought, I decided to revamp a couple from the recent past, add a couple of new songs and give them all a country rock feel. I also had a desire to paint, inspired by my project in Catalunya.

 I found a small studio in Teignmouth, run by Tony Carey, who became a good friend. He was a very talented, multi-musician and sound engineer, although we did have some issues regarding the final mix. Tony himself laid down the main tracks, piano, drums, rhythm, lead guitars, acoustic and electric with some mandolin for good measure. He also played a mean bass. His studio was in his converted garage, small but very functional.

In a previous chapter, I mentioned a certain Joe Meek. Well, Tony had some equipment of his built into the racks. On several songs, we needed to add steel guitar, harmonica, and sax, to give it that country feel. We used some extra guys for that and added backing vocals, with Colin from the Bovey Boys and another friend, Judith. I had recorded most of the nine tracks but still needed a saxophonist.

Tony rang me and said he had found a guy in Exeter, who was willing to come into the studio and play for me. We agreed a reasonable rate, and booked the studio, to meet him and go through my ideas, that only exist in my head. Two songs in particular, required a dominant sax sound, "*Rip it up* and '*Still Confused*'. A heavy rock and roll section for '*Rip it up*', for which we agreed a trio of sax, bass tenor, and alto and I had an idea for '*Still Confused*', a similar run to the sax sound on Cliff's recent song '*Joanna*', remembering the sax player in Belgium.

I explained the melody to Ray, the saxman, and we agreed to meet the following week to record the tracks.

He brought three saxes and had prepared sheet music based on my ideas. He did the rock stuff first. Boy oh boy was this guy good! I was literally on tenterhooks to see his rendition of the softer track, '*Still Confused*'.

He started playing and at once my hair stood on end. He could not have pitched it better; it was exactly what I wanted. The sound was perfect, the melody just as I had imagined, loosely-based on the sound I had heard at Cliff's gig.

 I was over the moon. When he walked out of the booth, I told him where I had got the idea for the sax part.

He laughed.

"That was me!"

"You?"

"Yes, me. I played for Cliff on his last two tours and I played for Suzi Quatro."

"Did you play in Belgium?"

"Yes," came the reply.

Thank you, Ray Beavis.

A year later it was obvious that relationships between Red's girls and their father was being rekindled. They were spending weekends together in Wales, he was spending money on them, they were enjoying the city life. In their teens, of course they loved shopping.

Our area in Devon was a little quiet compared to Swansea. Red would sometimes drive them there and stay with her parents. She once again became very homesick and she saw her parents ageing. They would all give each other support, and eventually she sat me down and told me she wanted to move back. The girls had made new friends there, plus they had their newfound relationship with their father.

She still loved me and I didn't want to lose her. She was deadly serious about this, so we sat down together and worked things out meticulously, one by one, with lots of compromises along the way. One major problem was that she did not have any interest in pursuing the Spanish project. The age gap between us was now beginning to rear its ugly head.

Relocating us all back to Wales would mean me living in my camper van three nights a week in Devon to continue with my work, and commuting to South Wales at weekends. Another hefty compromise. But I went along with it and we threw ourselves headlong into the move.

Our new house, built in the late 30s, on the Carmarthen border, was in dire need of modernising. It soon became crystal clear that my weekends would be swallowed up with DIY. In just a few weekends, I managed to make the dated kitchen usable, strip wallpaper from our bedroom and build some fitted wardrobes.

One particular weekend I was preparing for a house-warming party. My folks were coming down from Manchester for the first time. The visit would coincide with the local agricultural show. The show-ground was directly opposite the house.

 The garden was a priority. It was long with a small wall opposite the rear door. At the back of the garden, there was a small orchard. When it rained, it flooded the rear path.

I started laying concrete slabs to create a patio area and path to connect the house to the garden, hopefully diverting the rainwater. It was a Saturday afternoon. I had started at around 7am, working steadily, not stopping for a cuppa. I had a deadline to make.

Late afternoon, Red walked in, and made some remark about not doing something to her likening. Words were said, I snapped.

The build-up of stress from moving house, travelling, being fully-stretched physically, mentally and financially had finally got to me. Also, I felt completely taken for granted. I lost it big time.

I pushed past her, bundled everything that I could into the car, even my clothes out of the washing basket and left.

So there I was, driving blindly, my mind all over the place. After all the effort I had put into the relationship, what the Dickens had made me throw it all away in an instant? After nine years!

Okay, it hadn't been easy. I had become a stepfather to her two children. Admittedly they had got more involved with their own father over last three years, and the move back to Wales had resulted in them spending more time with him.

Had I really just wasted the last nine years?

Of course not. There had been lots of good times. So why had I left? Why then?

It would be months before I would actually begin to understand that I was heading for a full-blown nervous breakdown.

A few weeks went by. I thought I would enjoy the tranquillity of being on my own, living quietly in my motorhome, with no DIY or travelling. I had time to reflect on things and it was summer. (At this point no contact with Red.)

The camper was only two years old. It had a full bathroom across the rear, and was comfortable, with a good kitchen layout. I was parked on a very popular campsite, close to the office. The problem was, the site fees were expensive, and with a mortgage to think about for the house in Wales and money required to finish building in Spain, I needed to find a cheaper location for the bus.

A bit lost, feeling sorry for myself, I began dabbling online, trying dating sites. I began chatting to an artist and glass painter who had a shop in Polperro, a small picturesque fishing village in Cornwall. Her trade name was 'Daisy May's'. She had been a psychiatric nurse, before her artistic side had taken over.

During this period, I painted my first canvas and started writing a children's story book, 'The Polperro Kids'. Something to sell to the thousands of holiday makers who descended on the beautiful, unique village every summer.

For several months we enjoyed each other's company. We went to many music events, got drunk and she assessed me psychologically. She was a creative, fun-loving woman. I thank her for the experiences we shared, but sadly it wasn't to be.

It was high time I called in to see the lady, Georgena, at Indiopond fishery again. It was a lovely holiday complex, with fishing lodges, a large lake and woodland, only minutes from work. Georgena ran the dog grooming business and her husband the fishery. It was where I used to take Danny, every six to eight weeks.

It had been at least three years since then. Bless him, gone but certainly not forgotten. She remembered me and Danny with affection. We reminisced about him, how he used to bark continuously until I returned to pick him up. I mentioned my dilemma with the camper van.

"Well", she said. "There's no reason why you can't park your motorhome here."

She hesitated.

"However, I have just gone through an awful time with my divorce and my ex-husband is still here. But not for much longer. Do come back and see me again soon. "

Although it was a holiday destination, they did not have people in touring vans on pitches, they only let out their log cabins, so it would have caused unnecessary problems had she allowed me in at that point.

I left my card and offered a friendly ear if she ever wanted to talk. Having gone through my divorce, just a few years ago, I knew only too well it wasn't a nice time for anyone, except perhaps the bloody legal brigade.

A week later she called me and said she would like to meet. We went to a local pub in the nearby village of Lustleigh, had a drink and a good chat about life and dogs. The following week we had dinner out. Then I was invited for the evening at Indiopond. We both liked music which was an excellent start, and were getting on like a house on fire.

She bred dogs. I was introduced to Bronson and Ella, two wonderful Standard Poodles and Holly, a beautiful collie. It was good to have contact with animals again, especially with Standard Poodles. They are so intelligent. And there I was with two of them!

We spent another couple of evenings together at her home, where she cooked for me and we listened to music in the cabin, overlooking the small stock pond.

The following weekend we agreed I could bring the motorhome over. I thanked her and said how much I enjoyed her company. In fact, I was interested in much more than her company two or three times a week. But how to let her know without spoiling what we already had?

I needn't have worried. The feeling must have been mutual, because that evening it was Georgena who took the bull by the horns and plonked herself on my knee. We didn't waste any more time after that.

Ironically, apart from the odd weekend, that very night, the camper went into retirement!

Ironically Red called, the same week, Gemma had a party in Bovey with a school friend. We met, we talked, agreed on a future apart, although I know it wasn't the outcome she wanted.

Chapter 15

Catalunya calls

The day job was still going well, despite the construction business fluctuating. We continued to increase our market share. An excellent secretary and a gift for delegation also allowed me to get involved in the promotion and development of the fishery Indiopond, as well as continuing my build in Spain. Kaye, Georgina's sister, had been appointed to assist in the running of Indiopond. She also played guitar and sang very well. We had some lovely evenings making music and entertaining the residents. The mood at Indiopond was now chilled and happy, after the departure of Marcelle, Georgina's husband, and business was good.

Once a month I would make time to pay a visit to my little Spanish house on the mountain, to enjoy the sun and the tranquility of being one to one with nature. My enthusiasm rubbed off on Georgina, and when I suggested she come along, she jumped at the chance. I couldn't wait to show her my little piece of paradise, to see if she saw it as I, through the dust and decay, in its wonderful glory.

We flew from Stanstead, and picked up my trusty twenty-four year-old Mitsubishi 4x4. Miraculously, it started up first time. I had bought it in England for £250. It had been registered in Malaga and had originally been imported via the UK from Texas! I loved it.

The village, Ginestar, hadn't changed in five years. It felt like walking onto a stage set in the late forties, a sleepy, traditional, rural community, population around 500, the majority of whom worked the land, producing olives, peaches, almonds, and grapes. A white grape, Macabeu, was the local Cava. I would have about a thousand such vines on my land in the near future.

One main street runs the length of the village, with the church of St Marti in the central square Finished around 1745, it is steeped in history. An old fountain forms the centre of a roundabout where a second street meets the main one. There is a beautiful old villa standing proud on the corner and it is said one of the main buildings used to be an Embassy back in the 18th century. Large doors and ornate wrought-iron balconies still exist on several of the large houses, all in need of major restoration. If you study the layout of the village, you can see that the large houses or villas, probably owned by wealthy, successful land owners, were originally built along the main thoroughfare at strategic locations, and over the centuries, not so grand buildings filled the gaps. The Ajuntament, Town Hall, is one such building, yet with an architectural quality about it.

No new building work had been started in the village for many years. The majority of the villagers were farmers, and for them, building outside of the village was almost unheard of.

Ginestar was typical of most Catalan villages, and certainly there was a steady influx of expats moving in, both full and part time, taking over old farmsteads in the surrounding hills, the 'campo', or buying a plot of land and building on it like me, or simply going for an old town house. This hadn't seemed to affect the sleepy atmosphere however, or infiltrate the staunch Catalan tradition of fiestas. Lots of them.

The Catalan community are intensely proud of their roots, heritage and language. English is rarely spoken, even frowned upon outside major cities. If an expat wishes to integrate at all, then he must make the effort to learn the basics of Catalan and respect their ways. Or return home disgruntled and rejected. It's a one-way deal.

In Ginestar there were three small bars and the co-op bar with an attached village hall/theatre. It was a year before I discovered it. Another year before I knew we had a bakery and a fresh fish shop, both tucked away on side streets.

Expats instinctively sought out like-minded folk, others like them, struggling to adapt, and I was no different. We used to meet up in Bar Magaluf, a family run bar, where we would watch football on the TV and mingle with the locals. A great opportunity to integrate without hindering them. When Barcelona was playing, they would drop their stern, aloof manner and go mad when a goal was scored.

I was introduced to the village by Peri Borras, the only local who spoke English, which he used to his advantage by selling land. We all knew he was making a big profit but we were getting a lot for our money too. Win-win. We were buying 'The Dream,' a new way of life. At that time, anything up to a five-acre plot with a licence to construct a newbuild or reform an old ruin would sell for around £10,000. It seemed good value, in a wonderful part of Spain untouched by the bucket and spade brigade. Besides, Peri was always taking everybody out to different restaurants and buying the beer. Everybody got on fine - we were all pioneers.

The spit and sawdust feel of bar Magaluf had at some stage in the 60s undergone some improvement. The imitation woodgrain bar stretched a third along the length of the room, which was only fifteen feet wide, it had a brass foot rail. Suspended above five orange glass light shades, dangling via their own electrical cords. The shelves at the back of the bar displayed half empty bottles of spirits, some which hadn't moved since the Civil War. The walls were clad in hardboard, originally painted white, now, a rich browney-yellow, nicotine colour now. The floor, a white, flecked marble, tile, usually covered in cigarette butts, cream Formica-topped tables with grey leatherette padded chairs and about five bar stools, definitely from the 60s.

A large gin and tonic, and I mean a large one (a triple at least, UK standards) cost just one euro and a beer, 75 cents. We would sit out on the street most of the time and watch the world go by. It was no exception to see a tractor and trailer full of fruit and the odd mule trundle by. Noisy little scooters laden with baskets of home grown crops, strapped to the back would skid noisily by, emitting a trail of white smoke, as the peasant farmer headed home for his evening meal, dog perched on the handlebars - a regular sight.

A normal day for the farmers would start with a brandy or a glass of wine and a coffee in the bar, before heading off to the land. Lunch was a serious affair, to which they devoted three hours, again with some wine, returning to the fields until dusk. Then back to the bar for a quick one, before heading home for supper. You didn't have to worry too much about drink-driving. I am not advocating driving with alcohol in your bloodstream, but it was the norm. Extremely laidback, they would most likely look at you in confusion if you raised the issue. After all, they weren't jumping into their sports car and racing along the motorway every day. The local police were aware of the customs of course, and turned a blind eye. That was how things used to be.

But nothing stays the same forever. At first, there was a small select group of expats, from varying backgrounds, the vast majority moving into the area with the same pioneer spirit, looking for an adventure and a place to retire. Away from the rat race.

The attraction for Ginestar, apart from value for money, was the lack of outsiders. We were in the real heart of rural Spain, or I should say Catalunya. We wanted to change our lives. Unfortunately, too many Brits moved in, many of them on a shoestring budget with no viable master plan, hoping to sustain themselves by finding building work of some kind. They took advantage of the mayor, Josép, by ignoring the building laws and building illegal structures on rustic land, which went down like a dose of salts with the locals. It took time, sometimes years, to get a licence to build a 'vivienda', a house to live in. In the campo, plots of land, although cheap, only came with permission to build an 'almacen', store or animal shed, not for permanaent residence. This was a hurdle that few expats were willing to jump over. Seduced by the great deal of the land, the area, the realisation of their dream at arm's length, so close, they , more often than not, flaunted the law, and built anyway.

The authorities were not amused. Josép lost his position in the community after twenty-four years in office, to be replaced by a new, unscrupulous mayor.

Josép had been a decent man and a good mayor. He brought wealth into the area, money from the sale of lands, financed many improvements to the village, with a little help from European funds, which paid more as the population expanded to become eligible for grants.

The grants made new road surfacing, street lighting and a new town water system possible. There had also been huge investment into an irrigation network on the campo, helping to convert dry land into arable land, making it fit to plant, which in turn benefited the community.

Georgena and I spent a lovely week on the mountain, staying in the static caravan as the house wasn't ready yet. We had some days on the coast and I paid Hans, our German builder, some cash to continue with the internal brickwork and tiling.

The months flew by. My relationship with Georgena had gone up a notch, developing into a real loving partnership. We had an engagement party and my parents came down for a holiday along with my sister. We had lots of plans for the fishery, including a new website and a video. I was also drawing plans for some extra lodges and a house for us to live in, in the woodland.

Then we had a very dry year that changed everything. No rain and the construction of a hundred or so extra houses affected the five-hundred-year water level. Natural water courses that fed the lake ran dry. The water level was dangerously low. The old lake was also badly silted we had major problems, with the knock-on effect that both the fish and fishing were badly affected.

Georgena continued with her dog- grooming and I with my work, both under considerable stress. As a huge leap of faith and support, her parents sold their house and moved into one of the lodges. The business needed a cash injection, which they provided and subsequently had an equal say in the business.

Sadly, after all that, Georgena's father suffered the onset of Alzheimers, making things very difficult when decisions had to be made. The thought of living in Spain was becoming more attractive every day.

We discussed the situation seriously and during another visit agreed we would put my existing Spanish house, almost complete, up for sale. It was far too small, especially with a few dogs running around; we currently had seven. It was only a small 50sq.m footprint, the normal permission granted for an agricultural building on a single plot. We were stretching the rules, as it was, making it into a home. An extension would be impossible, so we made the decision to look for another plot of land and apply for planning permission for a larger building, with a view to moving over permanently.

It just so happened a few days later, Georgena and I were sitting on the roof terrace having a quiet drink, enjoying the sunset over the mountains. The sun set directly opposite us, disappearing behind the Templar Castle, high above Miravet, the village on the other side of the river. With views like that, I wanted for nothing.

Living on the mountain has its advantages. For one, you don't need a doorbell. The sound of an approaching car is a sure sign of visitors. There were two tracks up from the village, both almost impassable after a couple of hours of rain. Oh the joys of living on the campo.

We heard the sound of a car, and sure enough it soon came into view from the far track, over the ridge to our right. A blue 4x4. Four people got out. We waved in greeting, and then I saw who it was.

"Bloody hell, it's Alan. That 'parcela', plot, must be for sale."

They stayed only minutes before driving on.

The following day I stopped Josép the 'Alcalde', mayor, in the street. He spoke as much English as I hablé español, but we managed to communicate after a fashion. I asked him about land for sale.

"Bon día Josép mi Alcalde, ¿usted tiene una finca en venta, por favor?"

"Normando bon día, amigo," his arms open, smiling. "Welcome, welcome Georgeta."

He scratched his head.

"Finca, finca. Come." He made a gesture to get in his car and off we went. It was like going on safari with Josép. Good job he had a 4 x4. We headed off in the opposite direction to our present land to the west up a newly tarmacked road.

"Mira, Normando," "Look," pointing at the track now a road, then turning his finger towards himself. "El camino, Alcalde, bien. Good."

"Si Josep," I replied.

He was indicating he had arranged for the road surfacing. Quite a few English people had bought land up there over the last two years, hence the improvement to the road. Our track was a mud bath if it rained, but not very many people used it. I was one of the first expats in this area but all that soon changed. I met new people every day.

He stopped the car suddenly in the middle of the road.

"Normando." He was pointing to a small new building, then made a shape with his hands representing a roof.

"Normal correcto," (mono pitch) then another shape. (Double pitched) "No correcto."

"Me entiendo Josép, Correcto," myself now pointing.

We had had similar conversations before about how roof's should be constructed, what was right or wrong, what was allowed, as people had flaunted the law well outside the guidelines.

Then I said, "Josép, es possible un balcon?"

With a grin on his face he said,

"No balcon, que NO!"

I smiled, caught his attention again.

"Alcalde, es possible sóteno?" (subterranean)

"Normando, no. Sóteno, que no!"

He laughed. He knew I was winding him up.

I knew he was referring to problems with the interpretation of the building regulations I mentioned earlier. Both the ignorance and arrogance of the expats was incredulous. People would just do their own thing! It was as if their brains had melted in the sun. They would build underground storage and add balconies, to what was listed as an 'almacen', a store or an agricultural building. This would cause a lot of trouble and unnecessary heartache further down the line, sometimes going as far as the D word: demolition.

The first plot of land we saw was on the 'plato' above Ginestar. Three hectares, good access, water and 100 olive trees. He would give us a licence to build 95 square meters but only with architects plans, the only way to go after the recent problems.

"Precio Josep!" and with his finger in the dust of the car bonnet he scribed 30,000 euros then crossed it out.

"Precio Amigo!" then he wrote 27,000.

"Okay, bien," I said, at the same time trying to indicate that there were no views.

Then, with a wave of his arm, "Normando, Georgeta, come."

Off we went again, to look at two potential plots, but both high and flat with no views.

"Josép, ¿es possible una finca circa Baixantes?"

"Baixantees", he says softly to himself, while driving back down to the main road. "Okay. Baixantes que si."

We took a back road by the chicken farm, then turned into a small entrance, which split into several tracks, one leading to a large, freshly-ploughed field.

Josep jumped out.

"Ven," come, "bien, bien" he said.

Georgena and I were impressed. It had just been cleared of old almond trees, one hectare, flat and square. It was lower down the track than our existing plot, but with good views.

The price was good but he would only grant a licence to build a 50sqm structure.

"Lo siento," sorry. I shook my head.

 "No problem," said Josép.

We got back in the car, drove up the mountain over the ridge, looking at the panoramic landscape, our existing finca below us. It looked fantastic against the backdrop of the mountains.

He stopped the car, pointing.

"Mirais la vista! Baixantes, perfecto, Normando que si!" Look at the view. Baixantes, yes, Norman, it's perfect!

He went quiet for a moment, deep in thought.

"Baixantees," he repeated.

And suddenly we were off again, until drawing to a stop on a beautiful grass field, the car pointing down the valley to Ginestar.

"Esta es la vista, no?" This is what you mean, isn't it?

We jumped out of the car he threw his arms up in the air.

"Perfecto Normando, fenomenal!"

It was the land that people looked at yesterday.

With excitement in my voice, I said to Georgena,

"Oh my God, this is it!"

"Josép, el precio por favor?"

A crumpled piece of paper was carefully extracted from his pocket, whereupon he wrote down the price, with agreed planning for a 95sq metre build. Done deal. There and then. At that stage we were unaware that it also included a vineyard below.

Things moved incredibly swiftly after that. I was on a roll. I sold the existing house quickly and gave trustworthy Hans enough cash to begin work on the foundations.

This time it was unrealistic to suppose I could be hands on during the build. Back home, I had commitments I couldn't ignore and I had to be there. With this in mind, I sold the costly 4x4; the insurance alone was costing more than double the rental on hire cars. We then returned home to Indiopond, knowing it could be a long time before we made the move.

Chapter 16

One fine day, coming very soon

On Friday morning, 8th February 2008, while pondering over a cup of tea at the office, I was planning the logistics of the removal of classroom modules at Helston College in Cornwall. This included transport for fifteen wide loads and a crane, up through the narrow roads of Cornwall with, a final destination for most of the units being South Wales. There had been delays since the beginning of January, due to high winds. It was winter. Indiopod was on the market, but we hadn't had any firm offers. The move to Spain was dragging on and I wasn't feeling in the best of spirits.

My mobile brought me back from my musings, and at once I was alert, sitting up straight, eager to hear what the caller had to say. It was Mr Shaw, who had shown great interest in Indiopond, and had finally put in an offer.

"Please God, please God, let it go through", I prayed silently into the phone, as he voiced his approval. "This is a life-changer for us."

 He seemed happy with everything. The final hurdle was the inspection by the archaeological dept. to check out the site. Indiopond had been built on the ancient site of a monastery and could also have been part of the famous Bovey pottery! We often take history for granted, and Indiopond certainly had its fair share.

Part of the Bovey monastery, 'Indio lake' as it was called, was built within the curtilage of the 'In Deo Monastery' in the 8th century, during the reign of Henry II, after which it became a convent. The lake was known as the Pond Garden. Indio Priory, as it was then known, was dissolved by Henry VIII, and became a private residence in 1646. After a significant change of fortunes during the reign of Elizabeth I it was a refuge for the royal sympathisers involved in the Civil War, on the local heathland. Then it was renamed Heathfield. In 1775, Josiah Wedgewood came and stayed at Indio to investigate the competition at the Bovey pottery.

We crossed everything, hoping no relics would be unearthed and there would be no more delays.

The days dragged into weeks and then months. My fingernails disappeared, along with most of my patience. Would we lose the buyer? Was our dream just that? Was it meant to be?

The planning was granted after fourteen months. Fourteen months that seemed like a lifetime. So, when it actually happened, we were stunned. We had wanted it so badly, and after all the stress and doubt, at last, it looked like we were back on track. Dream on!

Worry, then disbelief, and then panic! Oh my God it was for real!

There were a million things to organise, from work to family and friends, let alone the practical aspects.

First things first. It was my responsibility to look after my staff and not put them in a situation that could jeopardise their future. Although I had given the managing director an indication, some six months ago when we had thought the move was imminent, everything had gone quiet. I had back-peddled like mad, to retain my position, saying the buyer had pulled out and that I would be around for another year at least. It was time to come clean.

And so one door closed, leaving us free to make plans to leave and find a new door to open. It was time to see how things were going in Spain. We decided to take a few bits over and pay a visit.

We hired a Mercedes Sprinter van, packing the van using every inch of space with literally everything but the kitchen sink. We sailed from Plymouth to Roscof and set off on what turned out to be an interesting although tiring drive, overnight, through France.

As the sun rose, we were granted our first site of the Pyrenees, majestic white peaks glistening in the distance through a band of low cloud. We had reached Gascony, having passed through Pau, some 16 hours after disembarking from the ferry. The weather was unsettled and as we drove on, rain clouds gathered, wrapping themselves around the mountains, totally blocking them from view.

We had been looking forward to our first trip through the Pyrenees, having seen photos, watching the miles run away, full of anticipation of the scenery, the fresh, pure air, the vastness, the magnificence and yet the simplicity of raw nature. And a few miserable rainclouds denied us all of that. The Pyrenees still had much to offer, however.

We came to a very narrow, steep, winding road. Funny, we had looked forward to driving through the mountains, without considering the state of the highways. In this day and age, I had taken it for granted that the roads would be up to scratch for modern day traffic. This was nothing like I had imagined. It wasn't suitable for commercial vehicles such as our van.

Had I taken a wrong turning? There was no chance of a three-point turn or reversing. We were stuck. Onwards and upwards, as they say, or bust! I gritted my teeth, slowed down and set my mind to negotiate the climb, praying we didn't meet any other large oncoming vehicles.

As we climbed, the clouds thinned out; we could see the tips of the mountains with large expanses of snow, lying in crevices that were shaded from the sun. The peaks towered high above, yet you felt like you could reach out and touch them. The sun's rays cast dynamic shadows across the cavernous valleys below and the lush green slopes, triumphantly came into view as the clouds dispersed. We were enchanted.

We passed by beautiful, isolated, stone buildings, none with any visible access. We climbed steadily on, up the twisty road for at least an hour, my heart still in my mouth at every turn, before reaching a plateau with what looked like an old abandoned border control building, with its rusty, bent barrier, just a hint of its original yellow stripes, the bar now fixed skywards to allow access to an open space with a sheer vertical rock face that encapsulated us. We drew to a stop, looked around in dismay, and my heart sank.

"Bloody hell, I think we are in an old quarry!"

I was furious with myself, relieved we had at least arrived in one piece, and frustrated, as it looked like we had wasted an hour risking life and limb on a dodgy mountain pass, to get to a quarry in the middle of bloody nowhere!

Silence from Georgena. Always the diplomat. What was she thinking? I reckon it's a woman thing. There are two types. Of course, every single woman on the planet can talk for England, but in certain situations, when all they can say will make things worse, they either go for the jugular and you end up killing each other, saying things you don't mean and wasting the next week or so not talking, or they zip it, sit it out and let things take their course.

Then, in the distance, I see what looked like the entrance to a small, narrow tunnel. More like a rabbit hole. Could that be the way out?

"We"ll never get this van in there. It's too high, for sure."

The options were limited. I certainly didn't fancy broaching the pass again. We had been lucky the first time. I didn't want to push it. So what should we do? Turn back, or breathe in and squeeze through the rabbit hole?

I could feel the panic rising in the pit of my stomach.

"Right, let's see where this tunnel leads", I said, far too brightly, switching on the ignition.

As we got nearer, a car suddenly shot out and veered past us. I could see the scale of the aperture and my eye caught a glimpse of a faded metal sign, hardly visible, above the arch.

'Max height 4M.'

I was committed. In we went, at once sucked into a black hole like a vacuum. I could see a small white, bright light in the distance. The walls had deep cracks in every direction, with green slime trails and water oozing from deep within the mountain itself. The ground was uneven, making the journey both bumpy and noisy. We continued downwards. The gradient was steep. It was like being in a sewer.

The small bright light, barely visible when we entered, had transformed into a powerful bright light, sparkling like a four-carat diamond, in a jeweller's window, as it reflects the intense light from spotlights, I could see blue shafts of light.

Was this actually going to be our first glimpse of Spain? ,

The road up to the tunnel on the French side had been very winding but when we shot out of the sewer, the road was virtually a one in ten and a straight drop, down the mountain. Ears were popping, as I applied the brakes hard, trying to control the increasing natural acceleration during the rapid descent.

It was like we had entered a completely different world, clouds to solid blue sky, as if someone had just flicked a switch. How could the light and the weather change in a fraction of a mile? It was like being reborn.

We were dropping hundreds of metres by the minute. I was in a low gear, the engine was revving to its maximum, I had my foot on and off the brakes as we cascaded along the narrow road, with deep potholes in abundance, caused by the winter freeze. The light and the warmth of the bright sun provided a boost of much needed energy.

There is literally was light at the end of the tunnel.

After around five kilometres and what seemed like a descent of 10,000 feet, we could see signs of civilisation. We passed lots of ski lodges under various stages of construction - timber structures! Not your typical build in Spain. It had never crossed my mind that people skied so close to my area in Catalunya.

Eventually, the road levelled out. We had been descending for a good hour. Suddenly, we came across a breath-taking view, a stretch of water, aqua blue.

Was it the River Ebro? We pulled over for a well-deserved break. I turned the engine off.

 Bliss, silence. I closed my eyes. For a moment, I thought I was in heaven until a passing car broke the trance. We opened the windows to feel the heat of the beautiful morning. Georgena walked across the road towards what could have been a mirage. We both stood for a while taking in the fabulous scene before us, our arms around each other, both thinking how lucky we were.

It wasn't the Ebro. It was a reservoir, formed by flooding a valley and consuming a village. Only the church tower was visible. The water reached the Ebro after flowing into Rio Cinca, which joined the Ebro at Mecquinenza, a mecca for fishermen, seeking the mighty catfish.

It was time to crack on.

I know now the route that we had taken was the D29, through the Tunel de Bielsa, down to Ainsa where the reservoir began, then on towards Barbastro on the A138. My main target was Lleida, a large city on the main route through central Catalonia from Barcelona to Zaragoza and on to Madrid.

When we reached the ring road, the traffic was wall to wall, due to major road works. It was a new junction joining two main highways, where everything came to a standstill. By then, temperatures had risen to around 25C. We were very tired, extremely hot and hungry. This was the last thing we needed. However, we had no choice but to sit in the traffic and crawl along.

The total journey time was a very long twenty-two hours. After clearing the traffic jam, we made good headway, following the more familiar route of the Riba Ebro, via Riba Roca, Flix, Garcia, Mora la Nova to Ginestar.

Fantastic. I felt like I was home. Well, I suppose I was.

We had a good night's sleep at the B&B in Ginestar.

The next morning, I wandered over to a friend, Paul's house, to ask for a lift to unpack the van. He was surprised to see me, and agreed to come over later.

 A Londoner, he had lived in Catalunya for seventeen years and all by default. He originally went out to build a house for a mate and then decided to stay. He married a Catalan woman Monsa, and they had a sweet son, Damaru, three.

We had known each other for a year by then. Together we were in the process of setting up an estate agency. Monsa had a lot of contacts, mainly family with land for sale.

We had spent many a lazy hour shooting the shit over a beer, revealing snippets of our lives, as you do. Paul had some right old tales about his infamous father, a bank robber, or rather, a would-be bank robber. He spent the most part of his life behind bars, so Paul and his little sister didn't see much of him while they were growing up.

"He used dynamite. One of the last of the old school," Paul told me.

We didn't know what to expect as we drove on to the land. It had been two months or more, unlike the first build, which I had lived and breathed at every stage of the way. This time round, although the design was mine, we had the local architect on board who re-drew the plans and presented them to the relevant authorities in the province of Tarragona.

The first thing I noticed was that a lot of earth had been moved away from the front of the main entrance doors, creating a terrace. Great, this would help divert water, which could cascade down from the higher ground and possibly flood the house during heavy rain. When it rained, boy, did it rain, sometimes for days on end.
I put the key firmly in the lock and turned it until the two Shute bolts retracted. We pulled open the large doors, allowing a little light into the first section of the house. My eyes took a few seconds to adjust from the external bright sunlight, as I stepped into the planned utility area or an area for making wine. I could even park a tractor in it when we got one.

I stepped down a level, walked into the lounge, past two bedrooms, and opened the second set of large barn doors, over eight feet high and ten feet wide, at the opposite end of the building, so that the light flooded in, providing the frame for a fantastic panoramic view down to the village.

It was a wow. There, right in front of us was the reason for building on that plot. We gazed up at the open vaulted ceiling, a feature making the interior stand out. The massive central timber beam supporting the large chunky rafters gave the sense of space. There had been progress with the electrics, and the plumbing had been installed, including pipes for the central heating system. Most of the internal walls had been rendered and wow, we had a shower room, as yet without a door. A plastic bucket sat under the outlet pipe.

"What's going on there?" I wondered. It turned out the main drain hadn't been hooked up yet.

"It's a flush it and chuck it!" Georgena laughed.

It was a joy to actually see that stretch of land and pile of bricks with a sketchy design be transformed into a home. Our home. We were just happy to be there. After all the hours back in the UK, looking for ideas, imagining what it would be like, painting the imaginary canvas of our lives, here we were, able to touch, feel and breathe the real thing.

We had instructions from Hans the builder to put all the things into the second bedroom, out of the way. We resigned ourselves to getting on with it and managed the smaller stuff relatively easily. Just the heavy, bulky items to go, lurking in the darkness at the back. A new enormous oak dining table, two very large sofas and the extremely heavy 9 kw super silent diesel generator.

As if on cue, Paul chose that very moment to roll up in his 30 year old Beetle VW.

Shame, it had been perfectly preserved for so long, garaged for many years. Those days were long gone, as it trundled up the bumpy track, clouds of dust everywhere, revealing several tell-tale dints and bumps inevitable in its busy, new life in the campo.

Paul saved the day. We even got the generator into the generator house in the heat of the day.

"Thanks mate, Couldn't have done it without you".

Standing up straight and wiping the sweat from his forehead with the back of his arm, Paul smiled.

"Glad to be of service. To be honest I wasn't sure my back would be up to it. It's been playing me up lately."

"Now you tell me"

I looked at my watch.

¡Olé! Most definitely beer o'clock! Let's go down to the village.

After several days we had achieved a lot, including having our new build signed off by the architect. Just in time as it turned out, as the new Alcalde, had stopped all building in the Ginestar province.

In many ways, this was a good thing, as so many expats had bought land, built on it, but had no real plans thereafter and were forced to leave when they couldn't manage financially.left unable to sustain themselves because building work has dried up. What did I say about the bucket and spade brigade? Let's add a trowel.

The exodus had the unfortunate knock-on effect of a small recession in the town. With a new mayor, the future was rather fragile and insecure. So many expats had ignored the piles of necessary paperwork and built illegally. How would he react?

As far as we were concerned, our house would be registered with the Land Authority, but not as a permanent residence, a 'vivienda'.

There were thousands of building all over Spain, used as homes
without the classification as such. It had been going on for years.

It was going to be a scorcher, as we prepared to return to Devon,
Already the temperature was around 16°Cc at only 10am. We had no
air-conditioning in the Mercedes, so the windows were down as we
made our way north-westerly towards the Pyrenees in the direction
of Andorra. We were allowing ourselves two days for the return
journey back through France, to enjoy some of the towns along the
way.

We had been on the road most of the day and were looking for
somewhere to park for the night. We drove into a small mountain
village. There were people in fancy dress, most of them with a glass
of something, an open air stage with a live band in full swing and a
fun fair with the local kids having a ball. We came to a halt at the
side of the road, a few hundred meters past the action.

 The funk/soul band, including a brass section, had about fifteen
members, bouncing around on stage, and sounded fantastic.

I wandered up to the crowded makeshift bar to order a beer,
forgetting I was in France. I ordered in my pigeon Catalan, which
got me a funny look from the young guy behind the pumps. The last
thing he expected at the local carnival was a foreigner!

I relied on his intelligence to produce the goods, after pointing.
Georgena and I literally had one sip of our drinks as the band struck
the last chord, there was a roar from the audience and that was it!
Fin.

Now the proud owners of a bag of potato waffles, we sat down and
watched the crowd slowly drift off. They had obviously had a good
day and we had just missed out.

I was extremely tired but the beer was very refreshing and soon I was eager to explore the locality, high in the mountains of France.

We walked around the remote village, Luzenac. It turns out it was built around an industrial complex that made Talc, talcum powder, (hydrated magnesium silicate), from crushed stone from the surrounding mountains, and was the main production plant for talc in the whole world!

Sadly, with no suitable parking area and the lack of a restaurant or hostelry, we reluctantly we moved on, both tired and very hungry

Five minutes away, we found Foix. What a pleasant surprise! The town was alive with people and there were banners saying something about a Jazz festival.

"Brilliant – it's tonight!" I said, as we drove into the main square.

I could see some motor homes parked there, a good sign and many restaurants, which had tables filling the pavements. A small roundabout divided this impressive heart of the town, with its historic buildings and magnificent castle with ornate turrets towering above the rooftops. I pulled into a parking area at the furthest point, towards the top of the square.

 I had noticed a lot of French policemen standing around, so I hoped stopovers were allowed. It was dusk. We had a quick clear up in the cab, putting certain things out of sight and arranged the back for our return, ready for sleeping. Using the water from a container, we washed our faces, ready to hit the town.

"Do we need a parking ticket?"

Walking over to a machine on the corner, I looked at the machine for a minute trying to work out what it said.

"I think it's free after 1800h, George."

Standing there slightly confused and probably looking very English, a guy passed and with a hand gesture, (a finger flicked across the throat!), said "Gratuit."

I understood that! As we started walking, hand in hand towards the action, I got a stern look from 'les gendarmes'.

"Bonsoir," I said with a smile.

He nodded and also smiled, or was it a growl?

The square looked fabulous, the streetlights casting an atmospheric glow over the scene, the castle's ramparts floodlit, the crowded restaurants with soft, coloured lighting and candles, providing a relaxing ambiance. Laughter, the sound of glasses tinkling and music filled the evening air. Perfect.

I noticed sections of road barriers, in various locations and a number of parked vehicles with bikes clamped on roof racks.

"Looks like the Tour de France has been through here today."

 "Really?" Georgena replied, "That's why the jazz festival is on maybe," with half a smile.

Thirsty and craving for a plate of French cuisine, we sat in a restaurant featuring a quartet of jazz musicians, not five metres from our table. The band included electric piano, drums, bass and rhythm guitar and the music was mellow. A waiter placed a menu on the table. A bottle of red wine was he promptly brought to the table, complete with a basket of fresh bread rolls.

It was a special night. We held hands as we talked about the day and enjoyed our food, listening to a young French woman, who entertained us with jazz ballads and some up-tempo songs supported by the band.

What a fabulous romantic evening, wine, women and song. Good title for a book!

Around midnight we made our way back to the van, settling down into our makeshift accommodation. Fed and watered, we were looking forward to some sleep, ready for the next leg of our drive.

Georgena soon fell into a coma! I was tired but struggling to relax; I was thinking about all the wonderful things we had seen that day and concerned about the rest of our journey.

However, I must have gone into a deep sleep too, as I was startled in the early morning by a repetitive, rhythmic metallic, clong, bong clang! What the hell was it? Georgena was still in a deep sleep. I had to get up and see, as the sound was getting closer.

 My eyes slowly focusing, not fully awake, I could make out yellow fluorescent jackets, moving around, erecting road barriers.

The penny dropped. - The Tour de France wasn't yesterday, it was today!

I had to think quickly. I looked closely at the barriers. I could see we still had access to the road, out of the square and I was now aware of guys on bikes already warming up. What a good job we hadn't parked at the other end of the square. If we had, we would have been sealed in. Just a few hours ago it had been filled with the tinkling of cutlery and piano keys. Now only the sound of steel barriers.

I slid the door back, "George wake up! Time to go. No time to explain."

I set off, dressed only in my boxers, Georgena pulling on her clothes as fast as she could. Over the next twenty kilometres, we passed hundreds of motorhomes and support vehicles parked alongside the road. I guess some two hundred cyclists as well, warming up and presumably heading for a starting point. Just like us, they were in for a long day. Goodbye, Foix.

The weather turned again for the worse, as we drove up through central France. We had a good run until we hit Rennes. It was about 4pm in the afternoon. Traffic was at a complete standstill. The bad weather plus the rush hour I presumed. Time to use the satnav for an alternative route. Big mistake!

We got lost. Two hours on, having been through pine forests, down roads so straight you could see for miles. Acres of the bloody things, planted regimentally, in straight lines that eventually merged into the distance. The sun came out, casting long shadows on the highway, glistening on surface water from the day's shower. A beautiful evening, but I felt shattered.

At this point, I didn't know where I was. I wasn't really bothered, the long day needed to come to an end, I saw a sign for a B&B.

 "Let's treat ourselves, George," I said, "Look there's the place over there."

We had been travelling for 14 hours.

It was a typical French country house with barn attached, set in acres of farmland, with mature gardens and a large, inviting, stoned driveway. It had pale blue shutters and the black slate roof reflected the evening sun.

 We stepped out of the van. Everything smelt fresh after the rain, the sun disappearing behind a backdrop of pines. The only sound was the birds starting to roost and the clicking of the exhaust as it cooled, - or was it my bones?

"You knock on the door," said Georgena,

I flicked the large, cast iron knocker on the solid, giant-sized entrance.

I don't know what I said when the door opened, but the mature, attractive French lady understood my request and replied

"Oui monsieur, juste pour ce soir?"

Watching the blank reaction on my face, she chuckled.

"Just one night?" she asked.

"Oui madame," I said with a sigh of relief.

Georgena looked first inside and then back at me.

"How much will it cost?"

Did I care? I was just glad to get out of that bloody van and into a shower. We were escorted to a room at the top of the house in the roof space, a large room with a Velux window, providing a view of the front gardens and beyond.

"Perfect, thank you," I said as I popped my head into the ensuite.

 "Oh, is it possible to eat?"

The last-minute request needed some thought, It was getting late.

She smiled. "Oui, monsieur 7.30pm."

"Merci," I replied closing the door to the room. We showered quickly, as we only had half an hour before dinner.

We made our way downstairs to the main living/reception and dining area, part of which had a full height open aspect, to the roof line, constructed with large old beams, lovingly cleaned to expose the pale pine. A fabulous stone fireplace dominated the main wall and a large table was laid for six people.

We were introduced to Monsieur Michel by Chantelle, the lady of the house and another elderly couple joined us at the table.

They were staying in the attached barn, or 'gite'. They were from Belgium. Very nice people and again, English was not a problem. Soon a three-way conversation was underway over a glass of regional wine. The chambres d'hôtes, had been totally rebuilt by Michel over many years and was now a popular place to stop in Callac, the village we had accidentally stumbled on.

The starter was a rich homemade soup, with freshly baked bread. Then we cleared a place for an extremely large bowl of steaming runner beans, the traditional 'haricots verts'. The ladies were presented with veal fillets on large china plates. Albert and I were also presented with two fine cuts of meat. Our hosts, in contrast, had two extremely small pieces of meat, obviously chopped from the end of the first two steaks. How kind! They had not been expecting two extra gueasts at their table that night.

"Help yourself to the beans, we have plenty, fresh from the garden," expressed Chantelle. We all responded in our individual languages.

I looked at our hosts feeling rather embarrassed.

"I am sorry! We have taken your food."

"No no! We are on a diet," replied Michel."

We both felt extremely uncomfortable about the whole situation, arriving late, then taking their dinner, but our hosts were undeterred and we sampled more wine until the cheese arrived.

We discussed our route, with our hosts and I was surprised when they said Roscof was further away than I had thought. We settled our bill, there and then, as we knew we would have to be up early if we were going to catch our ferry. We said goodnight and retired to our room.

We left Les Roseaux de Callac around 7am, programmed the sat-nav and set off through the fields of Brittany along the D15 to Quimper then the N165 towards Brest and on to Morlaix.

We stopped to refuel: sixteen cases of bubbly, four cases of white wine, six cases of red wine, whisky, gin, a bottle of port and some beer, because *One fine day,* very soon, we were going to have a bloody good send off to Spain.

Chapter 17

Excitement, pain and a Barcelona bus stop

All we needed now at Indiopond, was the archaeological report. Yes, we were still waiting to complete the sale.

Easter had gone, thank goodness, the usual English bank holiday weather, wind, rain and snow in some areas, making everyone miserable. I keep looking at the forecast in Catalunya. Lovely and warm there.

I had started to back-up the computer at Indiopond, as the computer and website would stay with the new owner. I also decided to set up a new website for my music. I had been telling everyone that Mr. Jay was going into retirement, so the scrapbooks were all out, and I spent the next few days scanning everything into the computer. It was good fun and it took my mind off things.

I was also enjoying my new hobby, painting. I was now improving considerably, with at least five canvases finished. One was an old door in Ginestar, another of the lake at Indiopond.

One evening, watching television, Graham Norton, was promoting a new show on the box The Ultimate Tribute Show.

I contacted them. It was a "look-alike, sound-alike" show. If you could sing like Sinatra, Elton, Cilla, Madonna, to name but a few, they wanted you. I emailed the link to my new website and the phone rang. The BBC gave me a choice of venues and dates.

Over the next few weeks, the more I looked in the mirror, the more I convinced myself that I was over the hill. I felt overweight, lethargic, old and past it.

'Just retire Norman', I said to myself.

So I didn't go! They rang me several times but I had made my mind up.

The ultimate tribute show ran for five weeks, but they didn't have a Cliff Richard! (If only!).

In anticipation of the move, we took a trip to Manchester to see my parents. By the look on my dad's face as he opened the door, he had obviously forgotten that we were coming. Mother went into panic mode. She liked to be organised, and there we stood on the doorstep, two Standard poodles in tow and all our luggage. It took a lot of patience, cajoling and three cups of tea to calm her down.

That weekend I caught up with my daughters, my sister, my nieces and my grandchildren, and went to the Lake District to see my friends in Ambleside. It would probably be a year at least before I got the chance again. The time flew and before we knew it we were back on the road home.

Mr. Shaw had been back in touch, asking for permission to transport one of the new lodges to Indiapond. I agreed, as it was one step nearer to completion.

During dinner with friends. I attempted to open a jar of pears in vodka. Using all my strength to free the screw top, I felt something twang in my groin, I had torn something. Days later, I was in agony, couldn't sit comfortably walk or lift anything. I couldn't believe it. Of all the times to strain something, especially when that something was down in the nether regions!

With all indications that completion was imminent, we arranged another trip to Spain on 24th April, Plymouth to Santander. My resignation ran out on 16th.. We loaded up an old transit and a large box trailer, on a mission to ship out as much furniture as possible.

I was still in pain. I had a blood test and an examination, and luckily nothing was seriously wrong. We did well, with lots of things packed tightly and no space left. We had already decided to return with the van and then take our personal stuff and the dogs, plus anything else we could fit in, on completion of the sale. However, I had bought the transit van with the intention of doing one trip only, as it was old and a bit suspect.

The archaeological survey and the technical side of the planning permission came through. We had the green light at last. Just the completion date to wait for.

We sailed to France again. The plan was to take as much as possible, enjoy a few days there and then head back for the final load, the final trip.

The new ship, The Pont Avon, was fantastic, like a cruise liner, with a roll-on roll-off design. A great improvement on the old ship, which had seen service in the Second World War.

We arrived bang on time in Santander, 9am Spanish time, and were soon well on our way, eating up the kilometres. Nine hours later, we were both straining to see through the windscreen in anticipation, as we drove up the hill to our house.

 I unlocked the big double doors. Although it was dark inside, as all the windows have shutters, we could see what a difference the tiled floors had made. I walked slowly through the main room to the large doors at the other end and opened them, so the light flooded in. It felt like a dance hall. What a fantastic space, what a transformation.!

We had the pleasure of spending our very first night in our new casa. Lit by candlelight, we poured a glass of vino, excited, relieved, full of dreams for the future. There was no going back, no second thoughts. We were both 150% committed and couldn't wait to be there permanently.

Georgena leaned over, caressed my arm and drew me to her. Everything felt so right, so perfect and it was.

We awoke early, around 5 o'clock to the sound of birds! On the roof, in the roof, everywhere! A dawn chorus like no other.

A woodpecker had bored a hole into the roof panel and through into the insulated sandwich boards to make a nest and, by the end of the week we had three more! The birds were using the roof like an airport!

 Before we knew it, our last day was upon us. We had arranged to pick up Paul and Monsa and bring them up to the house for a friendly drink. Later, Hans came too to talk about future work.

Driving them back down to the village, the van suddenly became hard to steer and then I lost the brakes! The engine stopped. I turned it over again but it would not fire up. It was dead, nothing.

We spent the rest of that Sunday afternoon trying to get the bloody thing going, with the help of Hans, who had worked for Ford, in Germany in another life, but it didn't help.

Plans now foiled, we had to fly home, just in time for the May Bank holiday Monday.

 It was a typically foul day. High winds and rain had persisted for the last twelve hours and was in for the rest of the day. Bev, my secretary called to say their tents had been totally wrecked in the high winds. She had gone camping with a friend to the coast.

I was sitting in the office at Indiapond, staring out across the lake, half listening to a film in the backgound, deep in thought.

My patience had long gone out the window with the gorgeous weather. The foul scene outside mirrored my feelings exactly. Time was ticking over, days were slipping away, and if we weren't careful, we would lose the sale. With only 4 working days left until the end of the month, we really needed to hear from Mr Shaw, the purchaser.

Our hands were tied. The ball was firmly in his court. All we could do was get more and more worked up, as the prospect of not selling and having to stick around loomed ever larger.

We had even started devising a plan B, relaunching Indiapond, with a fresh website. It didn't bear thinking about, but we had to face up to the possibility and be as prepared as possible.

The shrill ring of my mobile cut into my musings like a knife. I listened in disbelief, as Richard, the solicitor, calmly confirmed that yes, everything would be proceeding before the end of the month!

With all those black clouds around, there just had to be a silver lining. And that certainly fit the bill! Celebrations were never so welcome as that night.

With Plan A back on the table, I contacted Hans, who confirmed the transit had been repaired. I needed to collect it for our final trip. There and back, 2000 miles, 3 days. I put the plan to my Dad, hoping he'd agree to come along so we could spend some time together. We would fly to Girona airport, and take the early train to Barcelona, and another to Mora La Nova. He was only too happy to say yes.

In reality, things are never so easy. Girona airport turned out to be a small, uninviting warehouse, with nowhere to rest. Jeez, was it so much to ask? I stared out the window, and noticed a coach, with BARCELONA on the windscreen. Leaving within the hour. Decision made. Once in Barcelona, we would surely be able to find somewhere in Sants station to lay our heads for a few hours.

It was not to be. On arrival, we found it closed until 5.30am. Wearily, we walked the streets, amazed that nothing was open, no clubs or bars. We ended up on a park bench, and then upgraded into a bus shelter, munching on Mum's sandwiches. We had to laugh or we'd have cried! An 84 yr old and a rough-looking 58 yr old, with nowhere to go in the middle of Barcelona. Priceless! Dad took it all in his stride, bless him.

After what seemed like days, we arrived in Mora and headed straight for the bar for hot coffee. Hans came to pick us up, surprised and delighted to see my Dad. He gave him a gentle hug.

"Welcome, Mr. Jones."

We lingered over the coffee and warm croissants and finished off with a large brandy, before heading off to the garage to collect the van.

Hans went on his way, we bought a few provisions and went up to the house. After a few hours recuperating on the terrace in the sun and our bellies full, we headed back down to the bar early evening for a drink. We didn't hang around. We must have stayed in Ginestar about 18 hours, before climbing into the old transit for the journey back to Devon. As it turned out, airports aside, it was a wonderful trip. Quality time with my Dad was something that had evaded me for too long, under the pretext of being too busy; deadlines to meet, places to go etc. To this day, I am grateful for those precious hours we spent together. The return journey more than made up for the disaster on the way out. Visibility was great. We travelled through breathtaking countryside via Pamplona and through the edge of the Pyrenees. We saw the sun set together and a new dawn, before reaching the ferry port. Fond memories etched in my mind forever.

Chapter 18

The music never ends

I arrived home from an early morning drive to drop Georgina off at Reus airport. She was going to see her parents in England and an uncle, who was over from Australia.

Already I was bored. After just fixing up a Wi-Fi unit I had purchased that morning in Tarragona, I logged on and checked my emails, as always with anticipation. However, nothing special, just a few meaningless messages. What was I expecting? Maybe some response from a fan or a listener?

How can one, who has so much, feel as though he has nothing?

I received a text.

"Don't forget it is Cerys's birthday today."

Samantha, my daughter, reminding me.

"Shit, my granddaughter, she's thirteen today!"

I sent her a message on Facebook. She was online, so we said a few silly, meaningless things and I shut the page down.

I didn't feel that guilty. She probably didn't expect much from me anyway. I always forget birthdays and I rarely saw my daughters and grandchildren. It had been over 17 years since I had left them. At least now we had some reliable communication.

When I originally started to build halfway up a mountain, I never expected that technology would allow me to have the internet. We were running on a solar system that gave three-kilowatt hours and could even run air-conditioning at a pinch. We had an exceptionally luxurious, two-bedroomed, tractor shed! With pool and a vineyard.

The area around our abode had also grown into an oasis of greenery. Established olive, cyprus and palm trees swayed gently in the afternoon breeze, providing shade, thanks to an abundance of water. The water came from our irrigation system, which every plot had in our village, pumped from the river below to a reservoir, then fed via a network of pumping stations.

On the way back from the airport that morning, I made a small detour to Falsett, a nearby town in the Priorat, a world-renowned area for top quality wines. I wanted to drop a letter and a CD into the radio station. I walked slowly through the busy main area near the Town Hall. Some shops displayed their goods outside, trying to encourage people to buy local produce. The recession was definitely biting hard. I could see the entrance to the building closed off with a metal security gate. I couldn't believe the station was closed on a Saturday. That's Spain for you!

 On the wall on the right, there was a post box marked 'Radio Falsett', so I launched the packet through the gate into the air. It landed below said letter box. Airmail! I had marked it 'Urgente,' in the vain hope that someone would see it over the weekend and respond.

I was asking for an opportunity to do programs in English on their Catalan-only, radio network. I was already broadcasting on radio at Mora La Nova, only ten clicks away.

We had been living full time in Cataluña for almost five years. Where had the time gone?

We had both been so busy, finishing off the build, discovering the area, trying to learn a little Spanish and meeting people. We had even bought another property, a village house that we had partly refurbished, and rented out. It was our new holiday business venture, in Miravet.

Siesta time! I made a quick snack with a glass of wine, let the dogs out into our new shaded, fly-free courtyard and we all had a snooze; definitely the best option in 30°C heat with 80% humidity.

I drifted in and out of slumber, disturbed by the odd pestering fly that inevitably found its way into forbidden territory. My mind wandering, stimulated by thoughts, influenced by the fact that I was on my own for the first time in three years. Georgena and I had lived in each other's pockets, spent virtually 24 hours a day contentedly together, a true test of companionship.

Dozing, my mind flitted through the labyrinth that was my past. I was a failure, I decided. A complete loser. Just look at all the unfinished projects, the half-hearted attitude when I became bored, or lost interest if I didn't understand it. Look at the dozens of jobs I had ploughed my way through, involving machinery, cars, industrial projects, building design, construction. Employed, self-employed. Maybe it was because none of that really fulfilled me. Always reaching out for my ultimate goal: recognition.

It never once occurred to me that there are more ways to skin a cat. I was overthinking, and stressing out as a result. Coming at it from a different angle, all these jobs indicated flexibility, adaptability, proactive, energetic, making the most of the situation to provide for the family. Someone who did the right thing, sought out solutions, someone to rely on and trust.

With hindsight, I now see that such proactiveness was only in situations where I felt in control. Probing even deeper, I had actually had those moments in the past, where recognition could have come knocking, and my lack of self confidence got in the way. The time when I left a tape for Cliff with his roadie! What the hell was I thinking? After all the effort, getting close enough to chat and arrange to leave the songs, I didn't go the extra mile to hand it to Cliff personally, and then contact him afterwards for feedback.

Then again, the TV show. Too old? Past it? What was that about? Lack of self confidence.

So with that old chestnut hanging round my neck, ready to pounce when the big O, opportunity knocked, I was floored every time.

I only had myself to blame. Thank the Lord for Georgena, my soul mate. She built up my confidence on a daily basis, took me for who I was, who I wasn't, and tolerated my whims and behaviour when I tried to find out who I wanted to be. All this with a smile, understanding, acceptance, respect and love. My guardian angel indeed.

My mobile, this time thankfully, interrupted my semi-trance. Our holiday tenants wanting to view properties in the area.

Boredom long forgotten, estate agent cap fimly on, I sprang into action.

Later I decided to use the week to produce a CD of my songs, now that I had a studio. I had also been performing over the summer, after struggling to convince myself that I could still do it! After such a long break, I also had many restless nights caused by dreams depicting me in dressing rooms, getting frustrated with my sheet music etc. There was always a reason why I could not go on stage. Typical anxiety dreams.

I felt refreshed, in a better place, ready, with renewed confidence, thanks to some new musician friends. I had the bug back and realised that I should continue to follow my passion.

I used to have a quote on my notice board in the office, *Success is doing something they said you couldn't do.*

I was already active on the radio scene, in Mora and then La Cala. I was the only English person on radio in Catalonia, but was anybody listening?

A band from Bristol, The Shrinks, sent me a song,

'Nobody's listening, so we are all just pissing in the wind.'

I played it a lot!

Anyway, the radio station put me in touch with some guys and we formed a band, 'The Four Legends', later to be affectionately known as The Leg ends. On keyboards we had James Carter Stringfellow, from Wigan near Manchester. We had crossed paths before, without knowing it in the Northern clubs. He had been in a well-known band called Winston. On bass, Nico Majer from Holland, who had worked in music all his life, and Josép Cardonna, on drums, a Catalan, who loved his jazz. James (Jym) also sang himself; he loved Elton John's music and did some vocal backing for me.

Jym had a bar in Salou, so we practised there and did a show every Friday. Gradually we built up a following. At a vital point in our development, Jym had a major confrontation with the 'Salou Mafia' and the local authorities. The bar closed, after 25 years, the band lost its venue, causing untold upset with his wife. Poor guy, he had to find alternative income, so he joined the entertainment team on a cruise line and still today is sailing around the world.

Another 'If only!' Moment. Yes, if only we had stayed together, it could have been fruitful.

I was, as many, using social media. I befriended a guy in Scotland who was putting together a 'Shadows' instrumental band. I was asked to be part of it. It took me all of two seconds to accept.

 All my energy was focused on the new band. They seemed a good bunch of guys with some pedigree. Dougie Henderson on drums used to be in The Marmalade, a chart-topping 60s band, who called me 'Cousin Norman,' after the Marmalade hit of the same name. Then we had Davy Maddock, a singer-songwriter and fabulous all-round guitarist, and Billy on keyboards. All in their fifties, plus Gary, my contact, (Hank) lead guitar and Jeff was the bass player. He was the least-experienced, but nevertheless played very well. He was an architect, by day.

Thus, Norman Jay and The Delsonics, was born.

Maybe this could be it. The opportunity I had been looking for. The last chance.

I flew to Glasgow for a few days. We hired a studio and rehearsals went well, with a gig scheduled for the following month. Blue silk suits were on order and a pink jacket for me. Work on a sound and light system was also a project taken on by Gary, who had worked the Scottish clubs for many years.

We did the gig, our first ever performance and it was excellent. It could only get better, with time. Little did we realise it would be the one and only gig we would do.

Clubs had been suffering for years to survive. We were in the middle of another economic world crisis, and money was tight. Maybe Gary was aiming too high, asking high fees, but despite trying valiantly, he could not secure any further bookings. A massive disappointment, after all our time and dedication.

At that time, a TV phenomenon had invaded everyone's sitting rooms in the UK. *The X Factor* was great television and its popularity was spreading to other parts of the world. It was making its millions for sure.

I decided I would use the concept and produce a talent show in Mora la Nova, our main town. I got immense support from friends and the local ladies group, a great bunch of expats. We managed to convince the Llanterna Theatre to host the show and we made it a charity event, raising money for 'The Marathon', an annual Catalan fund-raising event for Cancer research. Posters were organised and the promotion was started for the first, 'Concurso de Talents' or 'M Factor.' The 'M-factor' reference was for the expats, obviously lost in translation, as The original X Factor was totally lost on the locals.We had previously done a successful show in the 'Llanterna' organised by a nice guy called, Jeff Gilvey, known as Mr. Swing. It included Amanda Malyn and The Four Legends, an all English cast, the first of its kind there.

I was determined to make the show as professional as possible, obviously not on a scale anywhere near the original production, but we had four professional judges, all involved with the music business. Isabel Cana, Director of a School of Music, Daniel Evans, an X factor finalist, Marcus, a UK entertainer and myself. We held a pre-show audition night and put through a total of fourteen acts, with a good mixture of ages and nationalities, which included a dance troupe, along with guitarists and singers. We also recruited female and male presenters, who spoke both languages to compere the show. I was interviewed on local TV, using a translator and we had good support on the radio networks, plus my own weekly show on 'Radio Mora La Nova'.

If I say so myself, it was a fantastic evening of entertainment with a good result. The winner was Farleigh Graham, receiving 250 Euros in prize money. We also raised a substantial amount for the charity. Farleigh, like Jym is now on the cruise lines and doing well.

So there I was without inspiration again, twiddling my thumbs and feeling a little low. February, my SAD hardly noticeable in Catalunya, yet still low moments.

Georgina was away again, visiting family in Devon, our parents in need of support, not getting any younger.

Left to my own devices, again dozing during a long, dark afternoon, I had another brainstorming idea. I most definitely shouldn't be left alone!

I was by then really into my radio, even producing a weekly programme for the 'Federation of Radio' in Catalunya, as well as my two regular FM stations, but without any feedback.

Why didn't I start my own radio station? Internet radio was the new media, part of the new concept, citizen news. I spent the next few days, matchsticks holding my eyelids open, investigating and learn the technology required.

'Radio Catalonia' was on air after a very frustrating week, a week in which my computer was almost thrown through a window several times.

Within two months I had it running 24/7, with seven other presenters producing and uploading programmes. A few gremlins got in the way, however. We pushed on but lost some listeners. A setback, but we did eventually get it all running to a very professional standard and with advertising too.

For more than a year, we were on air, when a DJ introduced me, via email, to his friend who developed websites. He said he would work free of charge and develop our existing website, It was a great opportunity.

He added a chat room and other apps, which slowed the streaming down. Not good! By helping me, he was actually causing disruption, which once again, lost us some listeners. I was now spending around sixty hours a week keeping the balls up in the air. I promoted it every way I could and started writing a full page in a monthly magazine, 'Catalonia Today' about the station, developed to give English speakers their own radio in Catalunya.

It was unique, a great opportunity but listening figures were only increasing in the USA, rather than in Catalunya, which was the whole idea. It was obvious that increasing listeners was going to be a challenge.

It is sad because I had the support of some great guys who produced programmes for me, each of them with a passion for music. They included *Davy Clincart, DJ Bubba (The Librarian), Dioasa Pagana (from Columbia) John Marshall (The Smersh), Walter Speeman* the talented *Big Dave Shirt*, who sadly passed away in 2015, and American author producer- presenter *Halli Casser-Jayne*, best known for her book 'Pyjamas with President Obama'.

I persevered for another few months, presenting live breakfast shows on weekdays. This however, intruded on my home life considerably, making me very unsociable, so with great sadness and regret, I closed it down.

I was asked to do another 'M Factor' at The Llanterna. I gave it a lot of thought but came to the conclusion that we just didn't have enough people to find enough acts in this agricultural area.

With this thought going around in my head, I approached the directors of La Cala radio. They liked it and we started to arrange another 'Espectaculo,' 'M Factor 2'.

Once again the response was excellent. We learnt from our first show, the format was similar except we eliminated performers sooner, so the running time was reduced. The first show with the interval was four hours, too long, so we cut it to three.

I had a long interview on TV, promoting the competition, which paid off because we had to add some fifty extra seats in the auditorium there were still people standing at the back. An undisputed winner again, this time, a young Catalan guy, presenting his own style of beatbox, collected a healthy money prize. The whole show was broadcast on local TV. I opened the show with an introduction in English and with the support of my dear friend Carolyn, also in Catalan, before singing an opening number. I believe the show was broadcast several times more over the following week. I was proud of my achievement, but without the support of friends and some radio personnel, it would have been difficult. That was 2013.

Around that period, a poster promoting my radio programme was noticed on a campsite wall. The visitor asked the owner if he knew the guy on the poster.

"Actually, I do," replied Ken Purkess.

Ken sent me a message to meet this guy, who passing through in his RV. He was from Canada.

On a steaming hot summer's day, he walked out of his RV in black trousers, black shirt, sporting shoulder-length, grey hair and boots. He looked very interesting.

"My name is Wil. Nice to meet you Norman."

He was a singer-songwriter, who now lived in Andorra, travelling and promoting his new album. He was interested in me and asked me about my radio programmes and I was pleased to help him promote his songs.

We became internet buddies, exchanging ideas over the next few years. In 2016 he told me he was arranging some songs with his friends, The Corrs! An interesting man Wil Hinkson.

As we approach the end of my autobiography, I am no nearer to creating that list of songs for Desert Island Discs, or indeed choosing an all-time favourite. Having never thought about doing it before, now seems the right moment. As I said in the introduction, I have been asked many times, if I have a favourite song.

So let me talk about a selection of artists with specific songs that did grab my attention over the last several decades.

Let's start with. *Dickie Rock.*

The connection to this guy is my Irish wife and an old LP her mother had.

Between 1963 and 1972, he was one of the frontmen of the Miami Showband (who were later in the headlines due to the Miami Showband killings incident). He had thirteen top ten hits with the Miami Showband, including seven number ones. Dickie Rock and the

*Miami were the first Irish artists to go straight into the number one spot with **"Every step of the way**," in 1965.*

Put it down as a favourite song of mine.

We have one.

'Every step of the way', a song that I still sing today, and have only ever sung it in acapella.

During his time with the Miami Showband, Rock attracted the kind of mass hysteria normally reserved for The Beatles, and in 1966 represented Ireland in The Eurovision Song Contest. Rock continues to tour to the age of 75 (2011), after a career spanning more than 40 years. Dickie received a lifetime achievement award in October 2009.

Now let me tell you about, *Harry Chapin*, introduced to me by a guy called Denis, who I used to chat to during my run, hosting nightly shows in that music pub near Smithfield fruit market in Manchester, during the 90s.

Harry Chapin didn't write songs. They were stories, so once you realised this, you were drawn in by the lyrics. He originally intended to be a documentary film-maker, and directed 'Legendary Champions' in 1968, which was nominated for a documentary Academy Award. In 1971, he began focusing on music. With John Wallace, Tim Scott and Ron Palmer, Chapin started playing in various venues in New York City.

Chapin was born into a middle-class family in New York City, the second of four children who also included future musicians, Tom and Steve. His parents were Jeanne Elspeth (née Burke) and Jim Chapin, a legendary percussionist. He had English ancestry, his great-grandparents having immigrated in the late 19th century. His *parents divorced in 1950, with Elspeth retaining custody of their four sons, as Jim spent much of his time on the road as a drummer for big band era acts such as Woody Herman. Following an unsuccessful early album made with his brothers, Tom Chapin and Steve Chapin, Harry Chapin's first solo album was 'Heads & Tales', 1972, which was a success thanks to the single. "**Taxi**."*

One of my favourite songs.

We have two.

*Chapin's only UK hit was "W*O*L*D", which reached No. 34 in 1974. His popularity in the UK owed much to the championing of BBC disc jockey, Noel Edmonds. The song's success in the US was championed by WMEX, disc jockey and friend of Chapin's Jim Connors, who partly inspired the song.*

On Thursday, July 16, 1981, just after noon, Chapin was driving in the left lane on the Long Island Expressway at about 65 mph (105 km/h), on the way to perform at a free concert scheduled for later. Near exit 40 in Jericho, he put on his emergency flashers, presumably because of either a mechanical or medical problem, (possibly a heart attack). He then slowed to about 15 miles (24 km) per hour and veered into the centre lane, nearly colliding with another car. He swerved left, then to the right again, ending up directly in the path of a tractor-trailer truck. The truck could not brake in time and rammed the rear of Chapin's blue 1975 Volkswagen Rabbit, rupturing the fuel tank as it climbed up and over the back of the car, causing it to burst into flames. A sad end.

His epitaph is taken from his song "I wonder what would happen to this world."

In America, remember me buying the album by *Eva Cassidy, 'Eva by heart'*, the debut album, released in 1997. It is the first studio album released after Cassidy's death in '66.

'Songbird', track six, must go down as a favourite too.

So that's three.

Bring on another female singer *KD Lang*. An album called 'Invincible Summer', went with me on a summer trip through France and Spain, in my camper, It's a wonder it still plays, I have played it so many times.

The song '**summer fling**' can go down as a favourite.

Number four.

Lang's career received a huge boost when Roy Orbison chose her to record a duet of his standard, 'Crying', a collaboration that won them the Grammy Award for Best Country Collaboration with Vocals in 1989. The song was used in the Jon Cryer film, 'Hiding Out', released in 1987. Due to the success of the song, Lang received the Entertainer of the Year award from the Canadian Country Music Association. Lang would win the same award for the next three years, in addition to two Female Vocalist of the Year awards in 1988. Lang was born in Edmonton, Alberta, the daughter of Audrey and Adam Frederick Lang. She is of English, Irish, Scottish, German, Russian Jewish, Icelandic, and Sioux ancestry. When Lang was nine months old, her family moved to Consort, Alberta, where she grew up with two sisters and one brother on the Canadian prairie. Her father, a drugstore owner, left the family when she was twelve.

I am not sure where *Isaac Hayes* fits into the list, but I had a very old cassette tape with songs I had recorded back in the 70s, and one song that always got me from this compilation was, '***The windows of the workd***'.

Put it in the favourites.

 So we have five so far.

 Funny thing is, they're all ballads.

Lyrics from the Isaac Hayes song:

The windows of the world are covered with rain,

Where is the sunshine we once knew?

Everybody knows, when little children play

They need a sunny day to help them grow tall,

Let the sunshine through.

   Nice..

This woman also came with me on my long summer trip, in my camper, *Annie Lennox, the album 'Medusa'.*

My favourite track?

'***The thin line between love and hate*.'**

Number six.

These songs are not in any sort of order of favourites, but I still don't know if I have one, that I could call number one.

Okay, *Sinatra,* Blue eyes, Bones, Frankie, whatever you called him he was the 'boss'. So many songs from great writers. All the male singers on the circuit, sang *'My Way',* including me. I would like to think I did it my way. *Paul Anka* wrote it.

'**My way**'. Why not.

We have a Number seven.

Frank also had an obscure album called *'Watertown'.*

Watertown is Frank Sinatra's most ambitious concept album, as well as his most difficult record. Not only does it tell a fully-fledged story, it is also his most explicit attempt at rock-oriented pop. Since the main composer of Watertown is Bob Gaudio, the author of the Four Seasons' hits Can't Take My Eyes Off of You & Walk Like a Man, and Big Girls Don't Cry, that doesn't come as a surprise. With Jake Holmes, Gaudio created a song cycle concerning a middle-aged, small-town man whose wife left him with the kids. Constructed as a series of brief lyrical snapshots that read like letters or soliloquies, the culminating effect of the songs is an atmosphere of loneliness, but it is a loneliness without much hope or romance - it is the sound of a broken man. Producer Charles Calello arranged musical backdrops that conveyed the despair of the lyrics. Weaving together prominent electric guitars, keyboards, drum kits, and light strings, Calello uses pop/rock instrumentation and production techniques, but that doesn't prevent Sinatra from warming to the material. In fact, he turns in a wonderful performance, drawing out every emotion from the lyrics.

I like several tracks on this but I am going for. '**What a funny girl you used to be**'. Number eight.

Number nine. This has been interesting for me, never having attempted to do such a listing. So nine has to be from my earlier years. I am not choosing a Cliff song. That would be too obvious.

 Let me go with a *Billy Fury* composition. He wrote some great songs. One album featured all his own compositions. It's relaxed and raw, *'The Sound of Fury'.*

'That's love', is great.

Make that number nine.

If I was doing a top 20, "*Miss you nights*, would be there, a *Scott Walker* track. 'These walls are too thin', and recently a guy called *Gino Vannellie,* who writes some cool songs, came into my collection.

 I especially like a track called '*Gypsy Days'*, and of course some Beatles songs would be there too.

Do I have a number 1 favourite song? Maybe.

The social media networks also introduced me to one of the original American DJ's on the radio in the New York and Philadelphia areas,

*Gene Arnold. H*e also started producing shows for my Radio Catalonia station. He was one of the originators of *'The Philly Sound.'* Gene was called Rick Roman in his early years as a singer and he gave me the song, *'Anytime anywhere',* a song he wrote for Frank Sinatra, which I put on my album, *'Recognition',* released by myself in 2015. Gene Arnold wrote and produced records under the

Rick Roman name for The Tridells, The Good Guys, The Stylettes, on San Dee and Worldwide Limited Records, and is an ASCAP Composer.

We had many conversations and during one, we talked about Cliff, who never made it in the US.

"Hey, my long-time buddy, *Charlie Gracie*, knows *Cliff Richard*, he has worked with him several times," he said.

I was intrigued and investigated, then about a year later I met Charlie near Barcelona. What a fantastic guy and a real Rock and Roll legend, having worldwide hits from 1957 and one of the first Americans to work in the UK.

One of his biggest fans is *Sir Paul McCartney*.

I covered an early hit of his, *'Butterfly'*, re-worked as a swing arrangement. It was also on my *Recognition* album. He liked it and played it on his weekly radio show, CRUISIN' 92.1 FM, WVLT, in Philly and gave the album a great review. 'Rock & Roll's Hidden Giant' is a new book about Charlie Gracie, acknowledged by Sir Cliff Richard, Sir, Paul McCartney and Chubby Checker.

Recently I did a radio interview with an American soul singer and songwriter *Sidney Barnes*. He was related to *Minnie Riperton,* who sang *'Loving you'*. I guess this could be my favourite song.

So 'Loving You', shoots to the number one spot, with the other nine in no particular order. My top ten list finally compiled.

My life in Catalonia has been sublime. I have so many friends and Georgena has been the best partner a man could wish for. We have sadly sold our beautiful tractor shed and lands, as the work was getting too much for us and I recently contracted pneumonia, which knocked my health backwards.

We are now, after a year of renovation, living in our townhouse in Miravet. Our parents are also requiring a little more support now and we have been travelling back and forth to the UK in our camper van enjoying the countryside in France each time we pass through.

I will reach the grand old age of sixty-seven this year and have decided that I have to somehow draw to a close my music career which has driven me for over fifty years. So, around the middle of January 2016, on yet another occasion when Georgena is away at her parent's house, I sent an email to Davy Maddock, a member of the Delsonics, that I was considering organising my final gig.

"I am going out with a bang," I wrote.

 "Okay, I will ask the boys if they would like to come over," was his response.

 I never expected that reaction but nevertheless, was so excited at the thought of a reunion. *As a performer you need an audience to bounce off. Let's hope we can do it one more time.*

 I am also looking forward to a show in Manchester, with the help of Pauline Renshaw, Strawberry Studios, first lady producer, who has worked with, 10cc, Godley and Cream, Sir Paul McCartney, to name just a few.

Let's hope it will be another One fine day, and I hope there will be many more days to enjoy in sunny Catalunya.

I feel thankful and blessed that I have achieved most of the goals in my life. Maybe a little more success in the music business would have been a bonus. I am very lucky to have a wonderful partner, fabulous friends, lovely grandchildren, and daughters. I am thankfully still involved with music, broadcasting and producing radio programs, mostly in the United Kingdom. I also have 1000s of watchers on YouTube. So you could say,

"The kid from Salford did okay!."

Recently I was enjoying the afternoon sunshine with a glass of vino tinto.

Feeling quite mellow and relaxed, a song started evolving in my head. I am at a funny age, you know. Soon I will only have my memories. I thought maybe it was time for the last song. Within an hour, I had it down on paper.

Lyrics, **The last song**

That could have been me tonight
Walking on the **Red Carpet.**
With the cameras flashing to the Rhythm of the band
I should have made it too
But my luck was always hiding
As I sang when important people were at hand.

You should have seen me tonight
Singing about my memories
Familiar pictures flashing
To the rhythm of my hands
I could have stayed with you
But I had to keep on trying
Something deep inside me
I will never know never understand.

I betrayed lied and cheated
To achieve the life I wanted
But my melodies don't seem to hit the spot
So this is my last song
And I hope I am never forgot.

I hoped and I prayed
As each night I put my life on that stage
That one day my name would be up in lights
But I am sad to say that I have had my day
It's time to say goodnight.

Daily Mail, *Aug 14th. 1978, 'Jet starts the long walk back from The Shadows'*

Manchester Evening News, *August 20th. 1978, 'Jet out of The Shadows'*

Manchester Evening News, *March 1979, Thursday Turntable by John Stacy*

'Jet back on the fame trail'.

Buxton local paper, *April 1979, 'Travelling light Jet Harris'*

Club News Saturday, *December 3, 1977,*
Norman Jay on Record.
Well-known around the local clubs as a talented
vocalist, he is also a first-class songwriter.
He has combined both talents to record his firt single,
'One Fine Day'. It will be released in the new year, on the
Pennine label.

John Needham, *studio director for Pennine says about Norman,*

"This lad is good and going places."

Manchester Evening News
Spotlight on Norman Jay 1976,
A young man with a nice, easy, relaxed style of singing is in constant
demand in the northern clubs.
Well known for his specially designed stage suit,,
considered flamboyant.
His act is styled on the great Cliff Richard but his voice has been
linked to Andy Williams and Buddy Greco, although he also sings Sinatra
classics and anything that swings.

George Bellamy, SRT records
"Norman's audiences have been captivated by the versatility of his
style and his clever re-arrangements blended with his original songs."

Radcliffe Times   1974.
Night out East Lancashire Paper Mill Club.
Great show hosted by Norman Jay, included Larry Stone and
Kathy Sampson.
Our picture shows Norman, 2nd on the right.

Manchester Evening News
January 6, 1978.
Matt D'Arcy's column.
New sounds could stem from Manchester with the combination of two well-known acts, Norman Jay and a four-man band Vintage, evolved from outfits like Dave Berry and the Cruisers and Johnny Peters and the Cresters.

Salford Journal
Local singer Norman Jay, 28, and his group Vintage have joined forces with a famous face of the sixties to form an explosive new act. Ex- Shadow, Jet Harris, has an opportunity for a successful pop career all over again.

City Reporter, *January 1978*
Norman has something to sing about.
'One fine day', has been released.
Written and composed by Norman, on the 'Pennine' label.

Manchester Evenings News, *December 1994.*
Diary by Andy Spinoza & Carl Palmer.
A Dream Comes True.
It was sheer bliss for Norman Jay singing along with his evergreen
hero in an empty Chinese restaurant, to an appreciative gang of kitchen
staff at The Pekinese Restaurant in Wembley, empty before they started to sing, I hasten to add.
Norman Major, Tim Rice, and Michael Barrymore having left a while
earlier, it was now 3.00am. We sang the Everly Brothers hit, 'Dream'.

British actors Equity Association
Application accepted 3/March/1980
Confirmed by Kevan Lim.

Strands Radio Helmond and Central FM
Voted Norman Jay's single, 'So Dam Distant', Number 5 on their Country Charts. December 2003

The Trader
September 2000
Norman Jay 'Radio is My future
"I think I could be the only English person on radio in Catalunya,"
said Norman, as he explained about The M Factor.

Salford Advertiser, *2008*
Clifton's Richard back after Summer Holiday.
A tribute act has proved he is wired for sound after more than 30 years in the business.
After retiring to Spain recently, Normans 'Miss you Nights' led him back to England to perform.

Catalunya Today Magazine, *July 2013*
Feature My Space. Norman Jay.
Resident in Catalonia for almost 5 years
Singer- songwriter launches 'Radio Catalunya'

"I always thought that Norman would make it big as a singer from moment

I heard him in the studio. Always a pleasure to work with and professional to a fault. **" John Needham, Music producer and director of Pennine Studios.**

"Norman Jay is an entertainer who thru generations, has pleased crowds
in many countries with bright, energetic music as both a presenter on
radio and in-person vocalist of great talent. I have been pleased to
know Norman and share airwaves with him over the years. A truly
talented man, I am proud to know"
Gene Arnold, veteran Radio and TV presenter and "The Sounds of Philly" pioneer.

"Always brought me the most challenging arrangements. I am glad to have been part of Norm's rich tapestry of ideas"
Lol Harris, Musician arranger Owner of Lolipop Studios.

Thanks for reading the book,

Norm..

O yeah, recently I did gig with the band again, Glasgow, then In Catalunya, in Miravet and The isle of Lismore Scotland.

57337444R00150